UPWARD LIVING

LIVING

in a

WORLD GONE MAD!

Surrender's Joy:

A Study of Philippians

UPWARD LIVING IN A WORLD GONE MAD

Surrender's Joy: A Study of Philippians

Published by

UPWARD LIVING PUBLICATIONS

ISBN: 978-0-9825175-0-5
Printed in the United States of America

Cover Design by Kevin Schreiber
powercentralmedia.com

TABLE OF CONTENTS

Introduction ....*i*

Paul's Mad World ....*iii*

WEEK ONE: THE SURRENDER OF UPWARD LIVING
PHILIPPIANS 1:1-11

Day 1 – The Church at Philippi (1:1) 3

Day 2 – Grace and Peace Be Mine (1:2) 7

Day 3 – He Will Perfect His Good Work (1:3-6) 11

Day 4 – Surrender's Real Knowledge (1:7-11) 15

Day 5 – Surrender's Discernment (1:7-11) 21

WEEK TWO: SURRENDER'S FRUIT
PHILIPPIANS 1:12-30

Day 1 – God Brings Good from Bad (1:12-14) 31

Day 2 – Christ is Proclaimed (1:15-20) 35

Day 3 – The Fruit of God's Peace (1:21-23) 39

Day 4 – Concern for Others (1:24-26) 43

Day 5 – Worthy Conduct (1:27-30) 46

WEEK THREE: SURRENDER'S HUMILITY
PHILIPPIANS 2:1-30

Day 1 – Humility's Unity (2:1-4) 57

Day 2 – Humility's Emptying (2:5-8) 63

Day 3 – Humility's Exaltation (2:9-11) 67

Day 4 – Humility's Application (2:12-18) 71

Day 5 – Humility's Examples (2:19-30) 75

WEEK FOUR: SURRENDER'S REJOICING
PHILIPPIANS 3:1-21

Day 1 – Rejoicing's Confidence (3:1-9) 87

Day 2 – Rejoicing's Righteousness (3:4-10) 92

Day 3 – Rejoicing's Focus (3:11-16) 96

Day 4 – Rejoicing's Pattern (3:15-19) 100

Day 5 – Rejoicing's Citizenship (3:20-21) 104

Contents

WEEK FIVE: SURRENDER'S PEACE
PHILIPPIANS 4:1-23

Day 1 – Peace's Foundation (4:1) 113

Day 2 – Peace with Others (4:2-3) 118

Day 3 – Peace Principles (4:4-7) 122

Day 4 – Peace Principles (continued) (4:4-9) 127

Day 5 – Peace with Circumstances (4:10-23) 134

Summary 140

Footnotes 141

Contents

Introduction
Upward Living in a World Gone Mad

Paul lived in a world gone mad … literally! The Roman rulers had a history of being corrupt, egotistical, immoral and mentally unstable. The status and appearance-conscious Roman society reflected their leader's sinful attitudes and actions, with negative impact on the family unit. They worshipped a confusing and changing assortment of gods and deities, with un-godlike characteristics. Their laws and regulations often resulted in criminals going free and good people being unjustly imprisoned, as was the case with Paul during the time he wrote Philippians (62 AD).

He wrote, not knowing whether the infamous ruler Nero would allow him to live or would sentence him to death. His purpose was to redirect the Philippians from a downward focus on a church conflict, back to an upward focus. He wanted them to walk their destiny!

Paul knew that an upward focus would lead to the complete surrender of every area of their lives to God. God's peace and strength would then sustain them in the midst of the present and future crises, difficulties and persecution. Moving from self-focus, they would be able to daily live their destiny and walk as light and salt in a world filled with darkness. A victorious walk would have to be a surrendered walk. There was no other way for them to walk in victory and destiny, and there is no other way for us.

Paul had met Christ many years prior, as a Pharisee—religious, yet lost. When he met Jesus in a blinding vision, he had been zealously trying to save himself by destroying Christians. As a result, Paul embraced the Christ he had persecuted, and his life was changed forever. In this way, Paul's **Walk of Surrender** began.

Surrender took Paul to places he had never been: intellectually, emotionally, spiritually and physically. Intellectually, he had to acknowledge God's truth and not lean on his own understanding and religious traditions. Emotionally, he had to learn to walk in **Surrender's Trust** and contentment instead of reacting negatively and fearfully to difficult circumstances. Spiritually, self-effort and control had to be replaced with God-control. Logistically, he had to learn to let go of some things that might be comfortable so he could fully live **Surrender's Joyful Adventure!**

God's plan requires our surrender to Him. It is a surrender that involves a daily death to self and an offering of our life as a "living sacrifice."

> ROMANS 12:1
> *Therefore I urge you, brethren, by the mercies of God, to present your bodies a living and holy sacrifice, acceptable to God, which is your spiritual service of worship.*

This is just what Paul learned to do, and this is how he learned to walk in **Surrender's** daily **Joy, Strength and Destiny.** In surrender, Paul came to a place in his life where he could say: *"For to me, to live is Christ, and to die is gain"* (Philippians 1:21).

ARE YOU UPWARD FOCUSED?
HOW SURRENDERED IS YOUR LIFE?

This is more than a book or study guide. It's a revolution of thinking and living! This study may be used as a companion to the book, *The Walk of Surrender*, which uses the biblical passage known as the Lord's Prayer to specify principles key to surrender, and further supports these principles by referring to specific verses, as well as my own story and the stories of others.

In contrast, this workbook leads the student on an in-depth journey* through Paul's letter to his beloved Philippians, written while he was imprisoned—chained day and night to a soldier. Throughout his correspondence, Paul urges his readers to rejoice, rejoice! In fact, the word *joy* or *rejoice* is found nineteen times in his letter!

Upward Living: The Walk of Surrender provides you with thought-provoking Word studies and devotionals to guide you in your own daily personal study. I urge you to complete the daily assignments, meditating on the powerful Scriptural truths that surface, as a way to enhance your daily time alone with God. In doing so, your own life and thinking will be revolutionized!

Get ready to live Surrender's Joy, Strength and Destiny!

Marcia L. Gillis

*This workbook may be used as a 6-week class study or a 5-week self-study.

Visit **upwardlivingpublications.com** for a free download of the *Upward Living in a World Gone Mad Leader's Guide.*

PAUL'S MAD WORLD

PAUL LIVED IN DIFFICULT TIMES, SOMEWHAT SIMILAR TO OUR OWN. HE AND HIS FELLOW CHRISTIANS FACED AN UNKNOWN FUTURE. THEY WOULD NEED EVERY BIT OF JOY AND STRENGTH THAT UPWARD LIVING PROVIDED THEM TO BE VICTORIOUS IN THE MIDST OF SUCH TURMOIL, STRESS AND UNCERTAINTY.

The corrupt egotistical immoral rulers of Rome had long used any means at their disposal to grab and keep their power—whether it was trickery, bribery, war or murder. They felt justified in killing those who disagreed with them. Their family lives were sacrificed on the altar of their political aspirations. Their power allowed them to participate in unbridled perversions. Their accomplishments included a mixed assortment of the good, the bad and the very ugly.

NERO, the emperor during Paul's time, was born on December 15, 37. He was the son of Cnaeus Domitius Ahenobarbus, a member of an ancient noble family, and Agrippina, a direct royal descendant. When Nero was born, his uncle Gaius had only recently become emperor. The family survived the short reign of the "crazy" uncle emperor who was soon assassinated. It is not unlikely that it took a conspiracy to bring about the rule of the next emperor, Claudius, another of Agrippina's uncles.

In 40, Domitius died, and Agrippina became a single parent, living as a private citizen until Emperor Claudius executed his third wife, Messalina. At that point, Agrippina competed to become the new empress, marrying her uncle in 49.[1] Soon thereafter, Nero was adopted by Claudius and the philosopher Seneca became his tutor, a relationship which endured for about twelve years. In 54, Claudius died after eating some mushrooms many historians believed were poisoned by Agrippina,[2] and the 16-year-old Nero was hailed as emperor by the Praetorian Guard.

During his early reign, this young emperor was strongly influenced by his mother, his tutor and others. The first five years of Nero's rule are generally described as a period of good government, as he focused much of his attention on diplomacy, trade and increasing the cultural capital of the empire. Agrippina never let her son forget that she had made him emperor.

Nero's marriage to Octavia, the daughter of the dead Claudius, was an important political step, but she was too shy and modest. He was attracted to another man's wife, Poppaea Sabina. At 21, he took steps to throw off the limits imposed by others by having his mother killed! Later, he arranged to execute Octavia and married Poppaea.[3] Nero's rule is often associated with tyranny and extravagance.[4] He is known for a number of executions, including those of his adoptive brother. He gained notoriety as the emperor who "fiddled while Rome burned" and as an early persecutor of Christians.[5]

The year 64 was significant. His mother and wife were dead, and Seneca had retired. Now, the primary advisor to the young emperor was Tigellinus, a man described as criminal in outlook and action. Nero set out to enjoy his limitless power and the advantages it offered. Essentially, the empire was at peace and the people enjoyed a full measure of food and fun—until a far-reaching disaster occurred!

The fire began in a shopping area and blazed for the better part of a week. It was controlled, briefly, but then started again. This led many to believe that the fires had been deliberately set. After about two weeks, the fire burned itself out, having destroyed ten of the fourteen regions into which the city had been divided. Though Nero attempted substantial relief efforts, many believed he was responsible. All his efforts to assist the stricken city could not remove the suspicion that "the emperor had fiddled while Rome burned." He lost favor even among the poor people, especially when it came out that a very large part of the city's center was to become his new home.

To bolster his failing popularity, Nero and Tigellinus realized that they needed scapegoats for the disaster. Christians, unpopular because of their refusal to worship the emperor, their way of life and their secret meetings, became the perfect scapegoat solution. Even more perfect, two of their most important "teachers" were in Rome—Peter and Paul.

The Mamertine Prison consists of two gloomy underground cells where Rome's vanquished enemies were imprisoned. Legend has it that Paul and Peter were kept here before their executions.

Christians were individuals whom most Romans loathed and who had often spoken about the end of the world. Their destruction was carried out with precision and cruelty in the guise of entertainment. In the stadium, Christians were exposed to wild animals and were smeared with pitch and set on fire to illuminate the night. The executions were so grisly that even the spectators showed sympathy for the victims. Tradition has it that Peter was crucified upside down on the Vatican hill. Around this same time, Paul was beheaded. As hard as he tried to cast blame in another direction, Nero was viewed as the arsonist and dissatisfaction over his rule grew. Eventually, after conspirators sought to displace and murder him, Nero committed suicide.[6]

Society's Sad Imitation

The Roman society reflected its leaders' sinful attitudes to varying degrees. The closer their city was to metropolitan Rome, the greater the impact. This impact was especially visible in regard to the health and stability of the family.

"The early marriage (449 BC) ceremony created a relation which the Romans called Hand *(manus)*, and brought the wife into her husband's power, giving the husband all the property she had when she married. It entitled him to all she might acquire afterwards, whether by gift or by her own labour. It enabled him to command her labour, and even to sell her, though the sale neither extinguished the marriage nor made her a slave, but merely enabled the purchaser to make her work, while still requiring him to respect her personal rights."[7]

Early on, divorce was frowned upon, but as more husbands began to put away their wives, it became more accepted. By Paul's time (60 AD), divorce was as common among Romans as marriage.[8]

Historians indicate that both men and women, especially rich women, were constantly changing their husbands, for the most frivolous reasons or impulses. To divorce, the husband just needed to say, "keep thy property to thyself" *(tuas res tibi habeto)*, and it was done. "Little or no social stigma seems to have attached to the divorcing partner, even to the wife, for public opinion, in older days a rigid guardian of hearth and home, had now, in a rich, luxurious, and corrupt society, a society which treated amusement as the main business of life, come to be callously tolerant." In spite of this disregard for commitment, there were still some examples of pure and happy marriages in this decadent society. Still the facts remain. There was a prevalence of divorce, the absence of social penalties, and a general recklessly wasteful, wildly extravagant lifestyle among the wealthier classes.[9]

Paul described his time period in **Romans 1:18-25**.

> For the wrath of God is revealed from heaven against all ungodliness and unrighteousness of men who suppress the truth in unrighteousness, because that which is known about God is evident within them; for God made it evident to them. For since the creation of the world His invisible attributes, His eternal power and divine nature, have been clearly seen, being understood through what has been made, so that they are without excuse.
>
> For even though they knew God, they did not honor Him as God or give thanks, but they became futile in their speculations, and their foolish heart was darkened. Professing to be wise, they became fools, and exchanged the glory of the incorruptible God for an image in the form of corruptible man and of birds and four-footed animals and crawling creatures. Therefore God gave them over in the lusts of their hearts to impurity, so that their bodies would be dishonored among them. For they exchanged the truth of God for a lie, and worshiped and served the creature rather than the Creator, who is blessed forever. Amen.

The Religious Background of the Roman Society

The Romans had many deities, including the most important Roman god, Jupiter, and countless numbers of secret beings and teams of minor deities (existing in extensive lists) each with a minor function in assisting or hindering in each activity or fraction of various human activities, particularly those characteristic of rural areas and those involving private life.[10]

Roman religion emphasized *pax deorum* ("peace with the gods")—the conviction that the basis for earthly prosperity was the maintenance of a harmonious relationship with the gods. In their perspective, all public disasters were caused by a broken relationship between the Roman people and the gods. The reasons for these breaks were diagnosed through divination and corrected by specific cultic measures. Peace was maintained by sacrifice and prayer, exact fulfillment of all vows and oaths, rituals and by paying strict attention to all outward signs of the will of the gods.

Divination played an important role in the lives of the Greeks and Romans up until the fourth century A.D. Divination is the art of interpreting symbolic messages from the gods. Greeks and Romans "distinguished between 'technical divination' (the interpretation of signs, sacrifices, dreams, omens and prodigies) and 'natural divination' (the direct inspiration of the *mantis* through trance, ecstasy or vision)."

The ancient Greek household practiced a cult which focused on the hearth and the tomb. "The hearth was the place where meals were cooked over a fire that was kept burning for an entire year. The male head of the household functioned as a priest, and such offerings were often made to deceased ancestors who had been made divine upon death. Offerings to these ancestors were also made at the site of their tombs, located on land owned by the family."[11]

During the New Testament time period, there was increasing tension between Rome and Judaism, and open hostility to Jesus and His teachings by the Jewish leaders (John 11:47-50; Matthew 24:1-2; Matthew 26:59-61, 66). During the time of Nero, the Jews revolted,[12] paying the ultimate price—the destruction of the temple and the ransacking of Jerusalem (70 AD).

The Romans disliked Christians, even more than they disliked the Jews. The Jews were thought of as an ancient people who had remained faithful to their ancestral traditions. In contrast, the Christians had left their ancestral religions to become followers of the Crucified Christ.

Christians refused to worship Roman gods, representing them as either nonexistent or demonic, and would not even acknowledge that others ought to do so (de Ste. Croix). To the Romans this was atheism.[13] It alienated the gods upon whom the well-being of the empire depended.[14]

Paul was fully aware that his pagan society recognized many gods and lords (1 Corinthians 8:5). The Acts of the Apostles and his letters, primary sources for our knowledge of Paul, show how the Greek and Roman beliefs impacted him and his missionary activities.[15]

POLITICS, LAWS AND REGULATIONS

The Roman Empire was monstrous in its size and reach throughout Europe and in its establishment of a trade route deep into Asia. During Paul's time, it consisted of 2.2 million miles and 60 million people, as many as one fifth of the world's population! 50,000 miles of roads spread Roman influence throughout the world.

Rome ruled its provinces with a strong hand. Though tradition indicates that Paul was killed by the Romans, Acts describes the Romans as rescuing Paul from Jewish hands, allowing him to continue his missionary work. One of his Roman imprisonments actually enabled him to travel to Rome and conduct missionary work at Roman expense (Romans 1:11-13; Acts 27:1-28; Acts 28:16)!

In the provinces, Rome allowed native leaders to rule and maintain order. It was these rulers who, initially, caused trouble for Paul. City officials imprisoned Paul and Silas in Philippi after they ministered deliverance to a demonic woman, therefore depriving her owners from their means of support (Acts 16:16-24). In Thessalonica, city officials were upset by the disturbance caused in opposition to Paul's ministry (Acts 17:8-9). In general, Paul was unjustly imprisoned seven times over his missionary activities, while others who were actual criminals went free.

Write down any noted similarities between Paul's mad world and ours.

_____

_____

_____

_____

_____

_____

_____

_____

_____

_____

WEEK ONE
THE SURRENDER OF UPWARD LIVING

Philippians 1:1-11

Day 1 – The Church at Philippi (1:1)   3

Day 2 – Grace and Peace Be Mine (1:2)   7

Day 3 – He Will Perfect His Good Work (1:3-6)   11

Day 4 – Surrender's Real Knowledge (1:7-11)   15

Day 5 – Surrender's Discernment (1:7-11)   21

UPWARD LIVING IN A WORLD GONE MAD
SURRENDER'S JOY
A Study of Philippians

"The cross must
be more
than a chain
worn around
our neck.
It must
be burned
into our heart."

Des Evans, Pastor
Bethesda Community Church
Fort Worth, Texas

WEEK ONE

THE SURRENDER OF UPWARD LIVING

What joy there is in beginning to understand the profound meaning of a passage and in allowing that meaning to infiltrate and change your life! This is just what you will see happen as you apply yourself to the careful study of the assigned passages. To aid you in the study, read the passages in your own Bible and in the sculptured/outlined format as they are given in each week's lesson. This format makes it easier to see the relationships of various parts of the passage to each other and key concepts. **Philippians 1:1-11** is sculptured below. Please begin your study by reading all four chapters of Philippians, and then the sculptured portion given here.

1 *Paul and Timothy,*

    bond-servants *of Christ Jesus,*

        *to all the **saints** in Christ Jesus who are in Philippi,*

            including the overseers and deacons:

        2 ***Grace*** *to you and **peace***

            from God our Father and the Lord Jesus Christ.

            3 *I thank my God*

                in all my remembrance of you,

4 *always offering prayer*

    with joy *in my every **prayer** for you all,*

        5 *in view of your participation in the gospel*

            from the first day until now.

    6 *For I am **confident** of **this very thing**,*

        *that He who began a **good work** in you will **perfect** it*

           *until the **day** of Christ Jesus.*

7 *For it is only right for me to feel this way about you all,*

> *because **I have you in** my **heart**,*

>> *since both in my imprisonment*

>>> *and in the defense and confirmation of the gospel,*

>> *you all are **partakers of grace** with me.*

> **8** *For God is my witness, how I long for you all*

with the affection of Christ Jesus.

9 *And this I pray, that your **love** may **abound** still more and more*

> *in **real knowledge** and all **discernment**,*

>> **10** *so that you may **approve** the things that are **excellent**,*

>>> *in order to be **sincere** and **blameless** until the day of Christ;*

11 *having been filled with the **fruit of righteousness***

> *which comes through Jesus Christ,*

>> *to the **glory** and **praise** of God.*

DAY 1
THE CHURCH AT PHILIPPI
Philippians 1:1

1 *Paul and Timothy,*

      __bond-servants__ of Christ Jesus,

            to all the __saints__ in Christ Jesus who are in Philippi,

     including the overseers and deacons:

The Philippians would have listened intently to the affectionate words of their teacher's long-awaited letter. As they listened, they may have tried to picture Paul in his imprisonment, knowing that he was more concerned about their well-being than himself and his own dire circumstances. It had been twelve years since he had seen them, yet this sentimental letter reveals that he had a special bond with this faithful church body.

It was during his second missionary journey (50 AD) that a dream, and Paul's **Walk of Surrender,** led him to Philippi (Acts 16:1-5), a Roman colony and a military and agricultural center initially established by the father of Alexander the Great. There, he met Lydia, a businesswoman. Lydia's conversion led to the conversion of all the members of her household, and her home became a base of operation for Paul's work and a place of assembly for the young church, one of the earliest to be founded in Europe.

Paul's work in Philippi immediately resulted in a beating and landed him in prison after he cast a demon from a slave girl (Acts 16:16-25). Her deliverance stopped the income her demonic activity generated for her greedy owners. Yet, what Satan would use for evil, God used for good. Prayer opened prison doors miraculously and the jailer and his family were saved (Acts 16:25-34)!

The jail where Paul and Silas were imprisoned.

Paul remained in Philippi only a short time, but this Gentile church kept thriving under the care of Luke and women like Lydia and others whom God was teaching to walk in **Surrender's Joy** (Acts 16:16-40).

Paul's writings indicate that the Church at Philippi had a prominence of women. In general, Macedonian converts were, as a class, very poor. This makes their generous financial support of the great missionary even more remarkable. They had often sent Paul money and gifts (Philippians 4:15-16; 2 Corinthians 11:7-10; Acts 18:5). Paul would only have been willing to receive money from friends with whom he had deep love and confidence, for he had a principle which absolutely forbade him to take such help from any others. Not only was he unable to refuse what his friends offered, but he knew he would never be misunderstood by them. In fact, the whole tone of Philippians reveals Paul's deep affection for the people of the Church at Philippi.

This is Paul's most personal letter. In it, he lays his heart bare, as he challenges them to be all they can be in Christ and updates them about his situation.

Bond-servants

Paul describes himself and his faithful co-worker, Timothy, as **bond-servants** *of Christ Jesus.* When you think of the word "servant," what comes to mind?

_____

_____

In this context, the Greek word for "servant" *(doulos)* is used metaphorically as one who gives himself up wholly to another's will (1 Corinthians 7:23); one who is devoted to another in disregard of one's own interests (Matthew 20:27; Mark 10: 42-45). The perfect example is Christ who gave Himself totally over to doing the will of His Father.[16]

How does the word "bond-servants" positively portray Paul and Timothy in regards to:

1) Their attitudes toward themselves?

_____

_____

2) Their attitudes toward Christ?

_____

_____

3) Their relationship with Christ?

_____

_____

Can you describe yourself as a bond-servant of Christ on a daily basis? Why or why not?

_____

_____

_____

Think of past circumstances from your life, one in which you joyfully surrendered to doing God's will and one in which you went your own way. Briefly describe these circumstances below, and contrast your motives, feelings and the outcome.

CIRCUMSTANCE ~ SURRENDERED	CIRCUMSTANCE ~ NOT SURRENDERED
MOTIVES	MOTIVES
FEELINGS	FEELINGS
OUTCOME	OUTCOME

Saints

Paul calls the Philippians **saints.** When you think of the word "saint," what do you think of?

_____

_____

In the Greek, the word translated *"saint" (hagios)* refers to people set apart for God; belonging to God, and as such, constituting a religious entity.[17] "It is important to avoid an expression which means 'sanctified,' for the focus is not upon a particular state of holiness, but upon a special relationship to God."[18]

We see many places in Scripture in which God gave His People new names. For example: Abram (High Father) became Abraham (Father of a Multitude). Sarai (Contentious) became Sarah (Princess). Jacob (Deceiver) became Israel (God Fighter). As Christians, we have been given a new name by God. We are called "Saints." The more we allow Him to control our lives, the more we live up to that name. We become Saints through our union with Christ. The more time we spend in His presence, the more likely we are to reflect Him to the world around us.

How does it make you feel to know that God has called you by a new name—Saint? Look up the scriptures below and write out other positive names that God calls you as His child.

ROMANS 1:7; 1 CORINTHIANS 10:14 »

EPHESIANS 5:8; MATTHEW 5:14 »

MATTHEW 5:13 »

ROMANS 9:8 »

1 CORINTHIANS 3:16 »

ROMANS 8:17; GALATIANS 3:29 »

1 PETER 2:5 »

ROMANS 8:15; 2 CORINTHIANS 6:18 »

GALATIANS 4:28 »

COLOSSIANS 3:12; TITUS 1:1 »

MEDITATE

Re-read this devotion and meditate on its implications for your life.

What is the Lord telling you? Is there anything you need to change about the way you think about yourself? If so, what is it?

_____

_____

_____

_____

_____

DAY 2
GRACE AND PEACE BE MINE
Philippians 1:2

2 *Grace* to you and **peace**
from God our Father and the Lord Jesus Christ.

"Grace to you and peace" was the common salutation in Paul's epistles. Grace was always first. Without grace, there would be no true peace. Inward peace comes only from a sense of divine favor, and comes through God's provision through His Son, our Lord Jesus Christ.

> JAMES 1:17
> *Every good thing given and every perfect gift is from above, coming down from the Father of lights, with whom there is no variation, or shifting shadow.*

Certainly Paul had every reason to be anxious and even bitter. Throughout his Christian walk he suffered seven beatings and seven years of imprisonment for no legitimate cause. His only offense was that He unashamedly proclaimed Christ and set spiritual captives free! Yet, in spite of such unjust treatment, Paul walked in peace and reminded his dear Philippians to do the same. He exemplified **Upward Living**!

Grace

Grace expresses God's unconditional loving-kindness/divine favor to sinful, undeserving people, like us. That amazing love was manifested in the life, death and resurrection of Jesus. Look up the following verses. What do they say about grace?

EPHESIANS 2:4-11

_____

_____

COLOSSIANS 2:9-10

_____

_____

ROMANS 6:14; ROMANS 8:1

_____

_____

Now meditate, for a moment, on what God has done for you. What do you have as a result of God's grace? Have you been living in the light of His grace?

_____

_____

_____

What do you need to change about your attitudes, perspectives and actions to live your life in the light of His grace?

_____

_____

_____

What would your life be like without Him?

_____

_____

_____

Peace

In Philippians 1:2 peace does not mean simply an absence of troubles or anxieties, but a state of total well-being, a wholeness of life resulting from forgiveness of sins and reconciliation to God through Christ. He is the One who revealed Abba Father as being the ultimate source of grace, but the extent to which that blessing is made possible depends on Him being confirmed as Messiah and exalted as Lord by His resurrection (Philippians 2:9)! He is also declared the giver of grace and peace. Through Christ we can have peace *with* God and the peace *of* God! **Upward Living** allows this to take place even in a world gone mad!

Billy Graham describes peace with God this way:

> Peace can be experienced only when we have received divine pardon—when we have been reconciled to God and when we have harmony within, with our fellow man and especially with God. "There is no peace, says my God, for the wicked" (Isaiah 57:21). But through the blood of the cross, Christ has made peace with God for us and is Himself our peace. If by faith we accept Him, we are justified by God and can realize the inner serenity that can come to man through no other means. When Christ enters our hearts, we are freed of that haunting sense of sin. Cleansed of all feeling of contamination and unfitness, we can lift up our heads secure in the knowledge that we can look with confidence into the face of our fellow men. "When a man's ways please the Lord He makes even his enemies to be at peace with him" (Proverbs 16:7). Even more important, we know that we can stand before God in the hour of our death with this same feeling of peace and security.[19]

Look up the following verses. What do they tell you about why you can walk in peace as God's child?

JOHN 14:27

_____

_____

ROMANS 5:1-11

_____

_____

COLOSSIANS 3:15

_____

_____

PHILIPPIANS 4:6-7

_____

_____

Even when the storm rages, our surrendered hearts can be at peace in Christ. Write out Philippians 4:6-7.

_____

_____

_____

_____

_____

We surrender to God, the One who so desired relationship _with_ us and good

for us that He gave His own life, paying the ultimate price.

He has proven Himself trustworthy!

MEDITATE

Re-read this devotion and meditate on its implications for your life.

What is the Lord telling you?

_____

_____

_____

_____

_____

_____

_____

MEMORIZE

Memorize the personalized version of Philippians 1:2 below, and repeat it every day.

Grace and peace are mine from God my Father and the Lord Jesus Christ.

Day 3
He Will Perfect His Good Work
Philippians 1:3-6

3 *I thank my God*
 in all my remembrance of you,
  4 *always offering prayer*
    *with joy in my every **prayer** for you all,*
5 *in view of your participation in the gospel*
  from the first day until now.
    6 *For I am **confident** of **this very thing**,*
      *that He who began a **good work** in you will **perfect** it*
    *until the **day** of Christ Jesus.*

Joy

The book of Philippians speaks words of encouragement to us, even as it spoke to the Philippian believers. Were Paul alive today, he would be saying to us, *"I thank my God in all my remembrance of **you**, always offering prayer with joy in my every prayer for **you** all, in view of **your** participation in the gospel from the first day until now."*

In some languages the translation would read, "Every time I think of you, I thank God for you, and I am continuously offering joyful supplication for you." Verse 5 provides the reason for the "joy" mentioned in verse 4: *"in view of your participation in the gospel from the first day until now."* The Philippians were imperfect beings, as are we, but they had continued in the Faith! Their lives had changed dramatically from what they had been—before Christ took charge. Without a doubt, though, they grieved over the areas of their lives that still needed change, just as you grieve. They needed to be reminded of how far they had come. Just as Paul said to them, he says to you, *"For I am confident of this very thing, that He who began a good work in you will perfect it until the day of Christ Jesus."*

Prayer

"The type of prayer Paul is offering here is supplication, the executive form of prayer."[20] It is as if Paul saw the divine intention and was praying it into existence. He saw that God had bigger plans for them than they could imagine for themselves.

Paul offered prayer for them with "joy," not with a heavy heart. In some languages, this joy would be translated as "my heart dances as I pray."[21]

Why could Paul offer prayer for them with "joy?" Find two of the answers in Philippians 1:3-6 and write them below.

1) _____

2) _____

The word *"participation" (koinōnia)* has also been translated as fellowship, community and partnership. In general, the Greek word refers to "participation in something with someone." The context seems to indicate that Paul is not just referring to their financial participation, but to their wider share in the work of the gospel, as evidenced by their personal proclamation of the gospel, their sympathy, their suffering and their generosity.[22]

Without a doubt, the Philippians were people like you. Certainly they lived in a different time period and culture, yet they had similarities. They were brothers and sisters, singles, husbands and wives, mothers and fathers, common laborers and business people. They faced crises and daily concerns about finances and time management. They were busy, at times stressed, living in a time of upheaval. Yet, in the midst of living, they proclaimed Christ to those around them. They showed care to those in need and they gave to the needy and to support full-time ministers of the gospel.

Write out some ways you can "participate" in the gospel on a daily basis:

_____

_____

_____

_____

_____

Now, let's look at the second reason Paul felt joy when he prayed for his beloved Philippians and why he would have joy in praying for you.

> For I am **confident** of this very thing, that He who began a **good work**
> in you **will perfect** it until the **day** of Christ Jesus.

A study of the Greek meaning of the underlined words will enhance our understanding of the meaning of this verse.

Confident, v. (peithō)

"To believe in something or someone to the extent of placing reliance or trust in or on it – 'to rely on, to trust in, to depend on, to have (complete) confidence in, confidence, trust.'" In many languages trust or reliance is "to lean one's weight on" or "to hang upon" or "to place oneself in the hands of."[23]

Good, adj. (agathos)

Agathos describes that which, being "good" in its character or constitution, is beneficial in its effect. For example, a "good" tree will bear "good" fruit. "The neuter of the adjective with the definite article signifies that which is 'good,' lit., 'the good,' as being morally honorable, pleasing to God, and therefore beneficial."[24] "What is upright, honorable and acceptable to God."[25] 'Pertaining to having the proper characteristics or performing the expected function in a fully satisfactory way – 'good, nice, pleasant.'"[26]

Work, n. (ergon)

Business, employment, that with which anyone is occupied; any product whatever, anything accomplished by hand, art, industry, mind; an act, deed, thing done.[27]

The result of someone's activity or work – "workmanship, result of what has been done."[28] Work, employment, task.[29]

Will perform; perfect, v. (epiteleō)

To cause to happen, with the purpose of some end result – "to accomplish, to bring about."[30] To bring to an end, accomplish, perfect, execute, complete.[31] A strengthened form of that verb, in the sense of "accomplishing." The fuller meaning is "to accomplish perfectly."[32]

Study the Greek definitions above, then write verse 6 in your own words replacing the word "you" with "me."

_____

_____

_____

_____

"Paul did not see Phillipi as an outpost, struggling to exist. He saw something bigger."[33] He was praying that nothing would prevent these Philippians from fulfilling their God-given destiny.[34]

God's business is to do good work, even in a world gone mad. God's work is always good work. God has done—and will do—a good work in you. "He will perfect it." He's not done with you yet. The more you focus on Him, His Words and His work, the more able He is to do His good work in you. Write out some of the good things He has done *in* you, *through* you and *for* you.

_____

_____

_____

_____

People of faith are people of prayer. People of faith are people of the Word. **Surrender's Change** demands faith and trust. It is easy to meander. "You don't need faith to go around the same old mountain. Most aren't afraid of a shaking boat, if it's in their living room!"[35]

God sees something bigger for you. Are you going to allow Him to do it? Jesus has a timeless love for you. He sees you as a person of destiny. Are you going to allow Him to help you walk that destiny on a day-by-day basis? "You are more than a person of past history (the 'good old days'). You are a person of destiny (today and in the future)."[36] Accept by faith that which is already reality with God.

Our kingdom is an insecure one, dependent on our limited ability to rule. His kingdom is an eternal one. In surrender, we trade *self-rule* for *God-rule*. It is a minute-by-minute, hour-by-hour and day-by-day process.

We surrender to God because we trust Him. He has already earned our trust by making the ultimate sacrifice and by what He has done for us in the past. What you are is not what you are going to be. Learn to live beyond yourself. Come against the negative world influences with a different Spirit—Him in you!

Allow Him to complete His good work in you.

MEDITATE

Re-read this devotion and meditate on its implications for your life.

What is the Lord telling you?

_____

_____

_____

_____

_____

_____

_____

MEMORIZE

Memorize the personalized versions of Philippians 1:2 and 6 below, and repeat them every day.

Grace and peace are mine from God my Father and the Lord Jesus Christ.

He who began a good work in me will perfect it until the day of Christ Jesus.

DAY 4
SURRENDER'S REAL KNOWLEDGE
Philippians 1:7-11

7 *For it is only right for me to feel this way about you all,*
*because **I have you in my heart,***
since both in my imprisonment
and in the defense and confirmation of the gospel,
*you all are **partakers of grace** with me.*
8 *For God is my witness, how I long for you all*
with the affection of Christ Jesus.
9 *And this I pray,*
*that your **love** may **abound** still more and more*
*in **real knowledge** and **all discernment**,*
10 *so that you may **approve** the things that are **excellent**,*
*in order to be **sincere** and **blameless** until the day of Christ;*
11 *having been filled with the **fruit of righteousness***
which comes through Jesus Christ,
*to the **glory** and **praise** of God.*

There was definitely a special bond between Paul and the Philippian believers. He felt completely justified *("it is only right")* in his warm feelings toward them, for they had worked along with him *("partakers of grace") ("in the defense and confirmation of the gospel")*. These believers had not been silent about their faith. They boldly defended the gospel, answering those who spoke against it. With their defense, they showed clearly *("confirmation")* that the gospel was true.

"I have you in my heart" has also been translated as: "You are always in my heart!"

Try to imagine the situation. Picture the Apostle Paul, chained to a prison guard, dictating his letter to another or writing it himself. As he moves, the chain sways back and forth, chafing his wrist. Periodically, he may have looked up, a smile on his face, imagining a previous time of fellowship with his beloved friends. He may have thought of the gifts they had brought and words of encouragement sent through Epaphroditus. In prison, he would have had an abundance of time to just think and write, and reminisce and write, and pray—they were in his heart.

Friends, God always has *YOU* in His heart! When He thinks of you, He smiles. He remembers times you have talked to Him and other times you have defended the gospel. God sees and knows you better than anyone else. Sure, He sees when you make mistakes, but He also knows the motivations of your heart. Take comfort in the knowledge that God holds you, tenderly, in His heart.

In using the words *"God is my witness,"* Paul was conveying solemn, intense, personal emotion. He knew that God was One who could testify to the truthfulness of his inner feelings. *"How I long for you all with the affection of Jesus Christ."* Though Paul was surrendered to God's will and rejoiced in his imprisonment, he felt lonely and longed for his dear friends.

Paul's main concern was for his friends, not himself. He prayed, *"That your **love** may **abound** still more and more in **real knowledge** and **all discernment**."* With these words, Paul was expressing his desire that:

1) **They might have an agape love (God's love).** He prayed that their love for God, each other and all men, might overflow. Love was the fulfillment of both the law and the gospel.

   Look up the following verses. Then write out a definition of agape love.
   (Galatians 5:22-23; 1 John 4:8, 16; 1 Corinthians 13:1-8; 1 John 4:7-21).

   _____

   _____

   _____

   _____

2) **That they might be a knowing people.** Their love was not to be a blind romantic love based on illusion and feelings.[37] It needed to be a practical love grounded on factual knowledge. We love God because of who He is and what He has done! We love our brothers and sisters because we see God's image stamped upon them.

Passions, without knowledge, lead to error in judgment and action. According to Romans 10:2, *"The Jews had a zeal for God, but not according to knowledge,"* and they were transported by it to violence and rage.

> *"He who knows little quickly tells it."*
> ~ Italian Proverb

Knowledge

What is knowledge? Plato described knowledge as "justified true belief." In the dictionary, "knowledge" (n.) is defined as: 1) The state or fact of knowing, or 2) Familiarity, awareness, or understanding gained through experience or study. [38] It is interesting to compare those definitions to the one given for "opinion."

Opinion

"Opinion" (n.) is defined as a belief or conclusion held with confidence but not substantiated by positive knowledge or proof. *Opinion* is applicable to a judgment based on grounds insufficient to rule out the possibility of dispute.[39]

An "opinion" is a person's ideas and thoughts towards something. It is an assessment, judgment or evaluation of something. An opinion is not a *fact*, because it has not been proven or verified. If it later *becomes* proven or verified, it is no longer an opinion, but a fact.[40]

Let's compare some examples of "Real Knowledge" and "Opinion" below, as well as the results of actions based on each example.

Opinion or "False Knowledge"	Result
No one could love ME.	An inability to receive love from others.
I'm not as good as other people.	Insecure feelings and actions.
I have to earn God's love.	A constant striving to earn God's love.
To worship creation is to worship God.	Judgment by God.
There are many ways to heaven.	A rude awakening at Judgment Day!

*NOTE: *The basis for all of the opinions above is faulty teaching, dysfunctional experiences or a misperception of other's actions.*

Look up the verses given as proof of the knowledge statements below.

Knowledge	Proof	Result
God made me special.	Matthew 10:30	Positive self-esteem
I am different but equal.	Romans 12:6-8 Ephesians 4:11-12	Positive self-esteem
God loves everyone equally.	John 3:16	"I am loved by God."
God's love is free, but must be accepted.	Ephesians 2:8-9 Matthew 5:16 1 Peter 2:12	"I don't have to earn God's favor."
There is only One God.	Romans 1:16-31 Psalm 114:4-6 John 17:3	A life built on truth's foundation
There is only one way to heaven.	John 3:16	The solution to man's sin dilemma

Look up the following verses and write a definition of "Real Knowledge."
Proverbs 1:7; Proverbs 9:10; Ecclesiastes 7:12; Proverbs 2:6; John 8:31-32; 1 Corinthians 3:18; James 3:14.

_____

_____

_____

_____

_____

_____

Real knowledge is based on truth and facts. This is opposed to false knowledge which is built upon opinion, theory, misconceptions, inaccurate information, popular notions, dysfunctional experience and skewed perceptions. Build your life, philosophies and theology on truth!

In the left column below, write down some false knowledge you might have had before you were a Christian. Then, write the true knowledge and a scripture it is based on.

False Knowledge I Have Had	True Knowledge	Scripture
_____	_____	_____
_____	_____	_____
_____	_____	_____
_____	_____	_____
_____	_____	_____
_____	_____	_____
_____	_____	_____
_____	_____	_____
_____	_____	_____
_____	_____	_____

Surrender's Joy is based on truth!

You must do more than listen to truth.

Truth needs to be IN you!

Recognize that you are a person of destiny, and act on it!

MEDITATE

Re-read this devotion and meditate on its implications for your life.

What is the Lord telling you?

_____

_____

_____

_____

_____

_____

MEMORIZE

Memorize the personalized versions of Philippians 1:2, 6 and 9 below, and repeat them every day.

Grace and peace are mine from God my Father and the Lord Jesus Christ.

He who began a good work in me will perfect it until the day of Christ Jesus.

I will walk in love and righteousness based on real knowledge and discernment of His glory.

DAY 5
SURRENDER'S DISCERNMENT
Philippians 1:7-11

7 *For it is only right for me to feel this way about you all,*

because **I have you in my heart,**

since both in my imprisonment

and in the defense and confirmation of the gospel,

you all are partakers of grace with me.

8 *For God is my witness, how I long for you all*

with the affection of Christ Jesus.

9 *And this I pray,*

that your **love** *may* **abound** *still more and more*

in **real knowledge** *and* **all discernment,**

10 *so that you may* **approve** *the things that are* **excellent,**

in order to be **sincere** *and* **blameless** *until the day of Christ;*

11 *having been filled with the* **fruit of righteousness**

which comes through Jesus Christ,

to the **glory** *and* **praise** *of God.*

It's interesting to note that Paul prayed not only, *"That your* **love** *may* **abound** *still more and more in* **real knowledge,**" but he also prayed for *"all discernment."* So, what is the difference between knowledge and discernment, and how does it affect us? Let's see what the dictionary reveals.

Discernment

"Discernment" (aisthēsis) is defined as "perception, not only by the senses, but also by the intellect; cognition, discernment."[41]

Webster's Dictionary – a power to see what is not evident to the average mind, stresses accuracy (as in reading character or motives or appreciating art), for example, the **discernment** to know true friends.

Below are some definitions we find on the Web for the English word "discernment":

- Understanding: the cognitive condition of someone who understands; "he has virtually no understanding of social cause and effect"

- Discretion: the trait of judging wisely and objectively; "a man of discernment."[42]

Webster's dictionary gives the following synonyms for *"discernment"*:

"Discrimination, perception, penetration, insight and acumen."

Discrimination

stresses the power to distinguish and select what is true or appropriate or excellent.

Perception

implies quick and often sympathetic discernment (as of shades of feeling), for example, "a novelist of keen **perception** into human motives."

Penetration

implies a searching mind that goes beyond what is obvious or superficial, for example, "lacks the **penetration** to see the scorn beneath their friendly smiles."

Insight

suggests depth of discernment coupled with understanding sympathy, for example, "a documentary providing **insight** into the plight of the homeless."

Acumen

implies characteristic penetration combined with keen practical judgment.[43]

Discernment is an ability to see the real meaning below the surface. Paul inserts another word in front of discernment—*all*. He wanted his beloved friends to have more than a little discernment. He prayed that they would have "all" (the highest level of) discernment! Certainly, the highest degree of discernment can only come from God's inspiration through His Spirit!

As we study Philippians 1:9 we want to also take a look at the word *"wisdom."*

Wisdom

God begins by transmitting His "knowledge" to you about something specific, generally through His Word. However, knowledge by itself is not enough. There must be understanding, or discernment, for that knowledge to be beneficial. Without understanding, you will not know how to use that knowledge in a real life situation. After you understand the knowledge you have been given, you need to have the wisdom to be able to use that knowledge or apply it. Here is where we see the difference between having mere "head knowledge" as opposed to transforming life-altering "heart knowledge." We have all heard some people described as being "book smart" but lacking the common sense and wisdom to be able to use that knowledge in the real world. For example, how would you like to be operated on by a doctor who had "book knowledge" but no real understanding of that knowledge or the wisdom to actually use that knowledge in an operation?!

It is only when you have real knowledge and understanding that you will have the wisdom to *"approve the things that are **excellent**"* (v. 10). Below, write out some words that are the opposite of "excellent."

_____

_____

_____

What are some excellent things you should approve right now? Are there other "mediocre" things you are being tempted to approve? What are you going to do?

_____

_____

_____

_____

_____

How do you want to live your life? Would you rather approve excellent or mediocre things? Now, friend, Paul's words can be used as a challenge for you.

> *"And this I pray, that your **love** may **abound** still more and more in **real knowledge** and **all discernment**, so you may **approve** the things that are **excellent** in order to be sincere and **blameless** until the day of Christ; having been filled with the **fruit of righteousness** which **comes** through Jesus Christ, to the **glory** and **praise** of God."*

If they had real knowledge and discernment, Paul knew that his friends would make decisions that could be trusted, or "judged worthy on the basis of testing."[44] Here, the word *"approve"* refers to the ability of the saints to sift or test a certain thing and thus to recognize its worth and put their stamp of approval upon it.[45] They would judge worthy those things that were more valuable (excellent). The result of this would be that:

1) They would be an honest, honorable, sincere people (Sincerity relates to truthfulness of actions and of the heart. Philippians 1:10).

2) They would be blameless or not causing others to stumble (Philippians 1:10; 1 Corinthians 10:32; Acts 23:1; Acts 24:16; Ephesians 5:27).

3) They would be fruitful, bearing the fruit of righteousness and good works (integrity, virtue, purity of life, uprightness, correctness in thinking, feeling and acting: Matthew 3:15; Matthew 5:6, 10, 20; Matthew 6:1; Acts 13:10; Acts 24:25; Romans 6:13, 15, 18-20; Philippians 1:11).[46] Fruits of righteousness come from God and are evidenced by holiness that comes from a renewed heart. Our right living brings glory to God (1 Corinthians 10:31).

Paul had indicated (1:4) that he was making *supplication (deēsis)* for them. He was praying that God's kingdom would be outworked in His people.

Twelve years had passed since Paul had seen the people at Philippi face to face. Paul was praying that the mind of Christ would be actualized through the Philippians, that they would be a model of the kingdom of God on earth. He didn't want anything happening in time to interfere with that. This is why he mentions the conflict.

Is there any thought, attitude or behavior that is keeping you from reflecting Him?

_____

_____

_____

_____

Surrender's Walk is a process. It results in a life lived to God's glory. It is rewarded with a victor's crown. It's made up of more than is happening to a person at a moment of time though, for "God does not take still shots. He takes moving pictures."[47] What we are dealing with now is just part of the picture. We want to walk today's destiny in the hope of the finish line—our hope of glory. That which Paul had endured was part of a whole movie. He had seen beyond the "now" and was committed to following God's pattern (surrender) and so was able to walk his destiny.

Now, repeat the following, and acknowledge it as a prayer for your life:

God, I want to love You and others more that my knowledge may be true knowledge based on real Spirit-inspired understanding, so that I will be able to discern truth and make God-inspired decisions and judgments. Then, I will be able to walk blameless morally and in all my relationships. As a result, I will bring glory to You and will reflect Your glory to those around me.

Paul's true knowledge of God birthed increased faith and trust.
This was the foundation of his surrendered life and
enabled him to walk his destiny.

MEDITATE

Re-read this devotion and meditate on its implications for your life.

What is the Lord telling you?

_____

_____

_____

_____

_____

_____

_____

MEMORIZE

Review the personalized versions of Philippians 1:2, 6 and 9 below, and repeat them every day.

Grace and peace are mine from God my Father and the Lord Jesus Christ.

He who began a good work in me will perfect it until the day of Christ Jesus.

I will walk in love and righteousness based on real knowledge and discernment of His glory.

THE EPISTLE OF PAUL THE APOSTLE

PHILIPPIANS.

CHAPTER I.

PAUL and Timotheus, the servants of Jesus Christ, to all the saints in Christ Jesus which are at Philippi, with the bishops and deacons:

2 Grace be unto you, and peace, from God our Father and from the Lord Jesus Christ.

3 I thank my God upon every remembrance of you,

4 Always in every prayer of mine for you all making request with joy,

5 For your fellowship in the gospel from the first day until now;

6 Being confident of this very thing, that he which hath begun a good work in you will perform it until the day of Jesus Christ:

7 Even as it is meet for me to think this of you all, because I have you in my heart; inasmuch as both in my bonds, and in the defence and confirmation of the gospel, ye all are partakers of my grace.

8 For God is my record, how greatly I long after you all in the bowels of Jesus Christ.

9 And this I pray, that your love may abound yet more and more in knowledge and in all judgment;

10 That ye may approve things that are excellent; that ye may be sincere and without offence till the day of Christ;

11 Being filled with the fruits of righteousness, which are by Jesus Christ, unto the glory and praise of God.

12 But I would ye should understand, brethren, that the things which happened unto me have fallen out rather unto the furtherance of the gospel;

13 So that my bonds in Christ are manifest in all the palace, and in all other places;

14 And many of the brethren in the Lord, waxing confident by my bonds, are much more bold to speak the word without fear.

15 Some indeed preach Christ even of envy and strife; and some also of good will:

16 The one preach Christ of contention, not sincerely, supposing to add affliction to my bonds:

17 But the other of love, knowing that I am set for the defence of the gospel.

18 What then? notwithstanding, every way, whether in pretence, or in truth, Christ is preached; and I therein do rejoice, yea, and will rejoice.

19 For I know that this shall turn to my salvation through your prayer, and the supply of the Spirit of Jesus Christ,

20 According to my earnest expectation and my hope, that in nothing I shall be ashamed, but that with all boldness, as always, so now also Christ shall be magnified in my body, whether it be by life, or by death.

21 For to me to live is Christ, and to die is gain.

22 But if I live in the flesh, this is the fruit of my labour: yet what I shall choose I wot not.

23 For I am in a strait betwixt two, having a desire to depart, and to be with Christ; which is far better:

24 Nevertheless to abide in the flesh is more needful for you.

WEEK TWO
SURRENDER'S FRUIT
Philippians 1:12-30

Day 1 – God Brings Good from Bad (1:12-14)   31

Day 2 – Christ is Proclaimed (1:15-20)   35

Day 3 – The Fruit of God's Peace (1:21-23)   39

Day 4 – Concern for Others (1:24-26)   43

Day 5 – Worthy Conduct (1:27-30)   46

UPWARD LIVING IN A WORLD GONE MAD

SURRENDER'S JOY

A Study of Philippians

Week Two

Surrender's Fruit

12 *Now I want you to know, brethren,*
that my **circumstances**
have turned out for the greater progress of the gospel,

13 *so that my imprisonment in the cause of Christ*
has become well known throughout the whole praetorian guard and to everyone else,

14 *and that most of the brethren,*
trusting in the Lord because of my imprisonment,
have far more **courage** *to speak the word of God* **without fear.**

15 *Some, to be sure, are preaching Christ even from envy and strife,*
but some also from good will;

16 *the latter do it out of love, knowing that I am appointed for the defense of the gospel;*

17 *the former proclaim Christ out of selfish ambition, rather than from pure motives,*
thinking to cause me distress in my imprisonment.

18 *What then? Only that in every way, whether in pretense or in truth,*
Christ is proclaimed; and in this I **rejoice,** *yes, and I will* **rejoice.**

19 *For I know that* **this** *shall turn out for my* **deliverance**
through your prayers and the provision of the Spirit of Jesus Christ,

20 *according to my earnest expectation and hope,*
that I shall not be **put to shame** *in anything,*
But that with **all boldness,** *Christ shall even now, as always,*
be **exalted** *in my body, whether by life or by death.*

21 *For to me, to* **live** *is Christ, and to* **die** *is* **gain.**

22 *But if I am to* **live** *on in the flesh, this will mean* **fruitful labor** *for me;*
and I do not know which to choose.

23 *But I am* **hard-pressed** *from both directions, having the desire*
to depart and be with Christ, for that is very much better;

24 yet to **remain** on in the flesh is more necessary for your sake.

25 And convinced of this, I know that

I shall **remain** and **continue** with you all for your **progress** and **joy** in the faith,

26 so that your **proud confidence** in me may abound in Christ Jesus

through my coming to you again.

27 Only conduct yourselves in a manner worthy of the gospel of Christ;

so that whether I come and see you or remain absent,

I may hear of you that you are **standing firm** in **one** spirit,

with **one mind** striving together for the faith of the gospel;

28 in no way alarmed by your opponents—

which is a sign of destruction for them, but of salvation for you, and that too, from God.

29 For to you it has been granted for Christ's sake,

not only to **believe** in Him,

but also to **suffer** for His sake,

30 experiencing the same conflict which you saw in me, and now hear to be in me.

DAY 1
GOD BRINGS GOOD FROM BAD
Philippians 1:12-14

12 Now I want you to know, brethren,

    *that my **circumstances***

        have turned out for the greater progress of the gospel,

            13 so that my imprisonment

        in the cause of Christ

    has become well known throughout the whole praetorian guard and to everyone else,

14 and that most of the brethren,

    trusting in the Lord because of my imprisonment,

    *have far more **courage** to speak the word of God **without fear**.*

Imagine how upset you would be if someone you loved was put in jail for sharing their faith. Definitely, Paul's friends were upset by his imprisonment. Little did they know the degree to which God would use Paul, even in such difficult circumstances.

God's plan is always bigger than the obvious. Often, we cannot see anything other than the problem staring us in the face, but God has something more in mind. He can even bring good out of what seems to be bad. **Surrender's Joy** comes as we learn to walk in trust.

Truly God used Paul in a miraculous way during his six years of imprisonment. Indeed, his circumstances turned out for the greater progress of the gospel, so that his imprisonment in the cause of Christ became well known (v. 13). Scripture records many times in which Paul gave testimony of Christ, as he defended himself before governors, kings, religious leaders, political leaders and guards. Some examples are given below:

1. Paul defends himself and his Lord before the Jerusalem Sanhedrin (Acts 23:1-10).

2. He testifies before two Roman governors of Judea—Felix and Festus, in Caesarea—as well as King Agrippa (Acts 24-26).

3. Paul speaks Holy Spirit-guided words to the men on the ship he was sent to Rome on and honors God before the natives of Malta where they were shipwrecked (Acts 27-28:13).

4. He witnesses to the soldiers to whom he was chained as well as the visitors who came to visit him (Acts 28).

The people who came to Christ because of Paul's testimony while in prison were people Paul may not have met otherwise. God took the ashes of Paul's situation and molded something beautiful. Hundreds and thousands of people were impacted by those led to Christ by Paul's testimony!

What was the response of Paul's "brethren" to his imprisonment? Fill in the blanks, below, by looking at verse 14.

14 *and that most of the brethren,*

   trusting in the Lord because of my imprisonment,

    have far more _____

 to speak the word of God _____ _____.

Why would the brethren have more courage as a result of Paul's imprisonment? (Put yourself in their shoes, and imagine that one of your friends had been so used of God in an unjust imprisonment.) Write your thoughts below.

_____

_____

_____

_____

_____

The worst that could happen … *DID* happen, and Paul was used in a greater way than ever before!

The word *"courage"* comes from the Greek word, *"tolmaoo"* meaning "to dare," or "to be so bold as to challenge or defy possible danger or opposition." Write about a situation you are dealing with. What will happen if you shrink back in fear? Contrast what will happen if you step out in courage.

_____

_____

_____

_____

_____

_____

_____

_____

Are there some ashes in your life? Just wait, He will mold something beautiful from those ashes! Tell of a time in which you have seen God bring good from bad.

_____

_____

_____

_____

_____

GOD IS NOT COMING FOR A CHURCH THAT IS JUST WAITING TO ESCAPE. IN HIM, WE CAN WALK AS VICTORS INSTEAD OF AS VICTIMS. WE LIVE IN A WORLD THAT OPERATES ON PRINCIPLES CONTRARY TO HIS PRINCIPLES, YET WE CAN STILL WALK IN OUR DESTINY!

We can walk in our destiny as a friend, brother, sister, student or worker. We can walk in our destiny at THIS time, in THIS world, in THIS job, in THIS situation, in THIS school! We can walk in our destiny in this minute, hour, day, week and year. The past is gone. Today and tomorrow is the stuff that makes up our destiny. **Surrender's Joy** requires that we stop living in past successes or in regret over past mistakes. It requires that we stop wistfully longing for tomorrow, allowing today's destiny opportunities to pass us by. Surrender your today's living to Him, and you will experience His joy. Know that He is in control today and will be in control tomorrow and forever.

Some version of the word *"rejoice"* or *"joy"* is used 19 times in the book of Philippians. Do you think Paul was trying to tell us something?

Rejoicing fuels a glow, while complaining destroys.

Rejoicing kindles the flame of the Christian's joy. [48]

MEDITATE

Re-read this devotion and meditate on its implications for your life.

What is the Lord telling you?

_____

_____

_____

_____

_____

_____

_____

MEMORIZE

Review the personalized versions of Philippians 1:2, 6 and 9 below, and repeat them every day.

Grace and peace are mine from God my Father and the Lord Jesus Christ.

He who began a good work in me will perfect it until the day of Christ Jesus.

I will walk in love and righteousness based on real knowledge and discernment of His glory.

DAY 2
CHRIST IS PROCLAIMED
Philippians 1:15-20

15 *Some, to be sure, are preaching Christ even from envy and strife,*

    but some also from good will;

        16 *the latter do it out of love,*

            knowing that I am appointed for the defense of the gospel;

        17 *the former proclaim Christ out of selfish ambition, rather than from pure motives,*

thinking to cause me distress in my imprisonment.

  18 *What then? Only that in every way, whether in pretense or in truth,*

        Christ is proclaimed; and in this I **rejoice***, yes, and I will* **rejoice***.*

           19 *For I know that* **this** *shall turn out for my* **deliverance**

    through your prayers and the provision of the Spirit of Jesus Christ,

20 *according to my earnest expectation and hope,*

    that I shall not be **put to shame** *in anything,*

      But that with **all boldness***,*

        Christ shall even now, as always, be **exalted** *in my body,*

          whether by life or by death.

Have you ever been hurt by someone's words or actions? Have you been disillusioned? If anyone had reason to be hurt or disillusioned, it was Paul.

Paul now speaks of two types of preachers, each with different motives. The first type is "pro-Christ" but "anti-Paul." They were jealous of Paul's notoriety and success, even in prison (v. 15). They were preaching from strife. In other words, they were argumentative, always fighting with words. They were preaching out of selfish ambition, wanting to bring distress to Paul in his imprisonment.

It's important to note here, that Paul does not dwell on their motives or the hurt their words, attitudes and actions may have caused him. Instead, he focuses on the positive: *"Christ is proclaimed"* (v. 18). Here is an example of where Paul "took his thoughts captive." Instead of being sidetracked by a disturbing and hurtful situation, he focused on the good and kept "running toward the prize."

Reconsider Paul's time and situation. Here he is—imprisoned, chained to a guard, day and night, for the cause of Christ, his future in the hands of the unstable Nero. And, to add insult to injury, he knows that some who are preaching Christ have wrong motives. After all that he has suffered for Christ, some are even jealous and trying to discredit him! How can that be? The whole situation is unfair! Definitely his situation is the stuff from which discouragement and disillusionment are made.

So often we try to make heaven on earth. The result will always eventually be disillusionment. Situations and people will never fully live up to our expectations. Only Christ can do that. This life will never be heaven. But, it is in **THIS** life that we are to be light and salt. We **CAN** walk in **Surrender's Joy** in **THIS** life. We can walk in our destiny in **THIS** life.

Write out the following verses:

2 CORINTHIANS 10:5

_____

_____

_____

PHILIPPIANS 3:14

_____

_____

_____

Describe a situation you are dealing with or have dealt with recently. How can you apply the principles gleaned from Paul's situation and the other verses above?

_____

_____

_____

_____

_____

_____

This is a good time, also, to allow the Holy Spirit to shine His light on your own motives. Let love be your own motive in proclaiming Him and doing good works.

Regardless of the motives he discerned in the two types of preachers, Paul rejoiced. *"What then?"* "It doesn't matter. I'm keeping my focus on what's important." *"Only that in every way, whether in pretense or in truth, Christ is proclaimed; and in this I **rejoice**, yes, and I will **rejoice**"* (v. 8).

In the next verses Paul states,

19 *For I know that **this** shall turn out for my **deliverance**
through your prayers and the provision of the Spirit of Jesus Christ,*
20 *according to my earnest expectation and hope,
that I shall not be **put to shame** in anything,
But that with **all boldness**,
Christ shall even now, as always, be **exalted** in my body,
whether by life or by death.*

Does *"deliverance"* refer to Paul's final salvation in the Day of Christ? Surely we can all rest in the knowledge of that future deliverance! Or, does *"deliverance"* relate to the apostle's release from prison? In view of the fact that Paul follows his talk of deliverance by saying, *"Christ shall even now, as always, be exalted in my body, whether by life or by death,"* I would like to relate Paul's discussion back to his rejoicing and propose the following interpretation:

*"My rejoicing in Christ shall deliver me from the despair of my circumstances,
so that in my circumstances I can have hope."*

Where is your focus? Are you rejoicing in Christ?

Paul's earnest intense deep desire (v. 20) was that he would not do anything shameful, but that Christ would always be exalted (honored) in his body (his whole being) through his life or death. Surely we exalt Christ when we live a life pleasing to Him, speaking boldly of Him and praising Him. Of course, when we blow it, He is also pleased when we come to Him in repentance and allow Him to cleanse and strengthen us for the next line of battle.

In the use of the word *"expectation"* we see the picture of a runner stretching his neck so he can be first to touch the tape. Paul was not allowing himself to be distracted by the circumstances, but dominated by Christ: "I am in jail, but I am in Christ. I am in jail, but jail is not in me." Here, maturity can be defined as the ability to look beyond circumstances (now) and see who and what you are in Him, knowing that your current situation is only temporary.

"Paul was not limited to his problems. He could see that he wasn't just linked to time. There is more than what we see with the naked eye. We really are people of destiny. Paul had hope because he was able to look over his situation and say, 'I expect ….' Paul's priority was that Christ be enlarged in him."[49] He desperately wanted to please the Lord. Who do you want to please, first?

MEDITATE

Re-read this devotion and meditate on its implications for your life.

What is the Lord telling you?

_____

_____

_____

_____

_____

_____

_____

MEMORIZE

Memorize the personalized versions of Philippians 1:2, 6, 9 and 18 below, and repeat them every day.

Grace and peace are mine from God my Father and the Lord Jesus Christ.

He who began a good work in me will perfect it until the day of Christ Jesus.

I will walk in love and righteousness based on real knowledge and discernment of His glory.

As Christ is proclaimed, I will rejoice.

DAY 3
THE FRUIT OF GOD'S PEACE
Philippians 1:21-23

21 *For to me, to* **live** *is Christ, and to* **die** *is* **gain***.*

22 *But if I am to* **live** *on in the flesh, this will mean* **fruitful labor** *for me;*
and I do not know which to choose.

23 *But I am* **hard-pressed** *from both directions, having the desire*
to depart and be with Christ, for that is very much better;

What do people live for? What is the purpose of life? What is to be gained by continuing to live? These are important questions that many seldom ask themselves. A survey by Barna Research in May of 2005 provides some interesting insight as to where Americans place the importance of faith.

> The second-most common life priority, listed by 18% of all adults, was that of understanding and carrying out the principles of their faith. Again, women were more likely than men to list this emphasis (22% versus 14%). Adults in the 40–70 age group were much more likely than younger adults to prioritize faith (21% versus 14%). Not surprisingly, residents of southern states were more likely to list faithful living on top, but residents of the western states were equally likely to do so (19%) while people in the Northeast and Midwest lagged (15% in each region). African-Americans were the ethnic group most prone to prioritizing their faith focus (24%), while Asian-Americans were the least likely (12%).
>
> Evangelical Christians, who comprise just 7% of the adult public, were the ones of the few population segments to place a faith-based lifestyle at the top of the list. Almost six out of ten evangelicals (59%) did so, which was double the percentage of non-evangelical born-again Christians who followed suit (27%). Just 12% of the Americans aligned with a faith other than Christianity said living their faith principles was their highest priority. About one-quarter of Protestants chose this pursuit (26%), which was nearly four times the percentage of Catholics who did so (7%).[50]

What do YOU live for? What do you see is the purpose of YOUR life? What is gained by continuing to live? How do your views compare with Paul's and with other scriptural teachings? Read the verses below. Then, write out your primary God-given purpose.

Colossians 1:16-17
For by Him all things were created, both in the heavens and on earth, visible and invisible, whether thrones or dominions or rulers or authorities—all things have been created by Him and for Him. And He is before all things, and in Him all things hold together.

Proverbs 19:21
Many are the plans in a man's heart, but the counsel (purpose) of the Lord, it will stand.

Exodus 9:16
But, indeed, for this cause I have allowed you to remain, in order to show you My power, and in order to proclaim My name through all the earth.

Ecclesiastes 3:11 (AMP)
He has made everything appropriate in its time. He has also set eternity in their heart, [a divinely implanted sense of a purpose working through the ages which nothing under the sun but God alone can satisfy] yet so that man will not find out the work which God has done from the beginning even to the end.

Ephesians 1:5 (AMP)
For He foreordained us (destined us, planned in love for us) to be adopted (revealed) as His own children through Jesus Christ, in accordance with the purpose of His will [because it pleased Him and was His kind intent].

Matthew 22:37-40
And He said to him, "'You shall love the Lord your God with all your heart, and with all your soul, and with all your mind.' This is the great and foremost commandment. The second is like it, 'You shall love your neighbor as yourself.' On these two commandments depend the whole Law and the Prophets."

1 John 2:17
And the world passes away and disappears, and with it the forbidden cravings (the passionate desires, the lust) of it; but he who does the will of God and carries out His purposes in his life abides (remains) forever.

Hebrews 11:6

And without faith it is impossible to please Him, for he who comes to God must believe that He is, and that He is a rewarder of those who seek Him.

Matthew 16:25-27

"For whoever wishes to save his life shall lose it; but whoever loses his life for My sake shall find it. For what will a man be profited, if he gains the whole world, and forfeits his soul? Or what will a man give in exchange for his soul?"

2 Corinthians 5:17-21

Now all these things are from God, who reconciled us to Himself through Christ, and gave us the ministry of reconciliation, namely, that God was in Christ reconciling the world to Himself, not counting their trespasses against them, and He has committed to us the word of reconciliation. Therefore, we are ambassadors for Christ, as though God were entreating through us; we beg you on behalf of Christ, be reconciled to God.

My primary God-given purpose is ...

_____

_____

_____

_____

_____

I need to make the following changes to reflect my primary God-given purpose in the way I live my life:

_____

_____

_____

_____

_____

_____

_____

MEDITATE

Re-read this devotion and meditate on its implications for your life.

What is the Lord telling you?

_____

_____

_____

_____

_____

_____

_____

MEMORIZE

Memorize the personalized versions of Philippians 1:2, 6, 9, 18 and 21 below, and repeat them every day.

Grace and peace are mine from God my Father and the Lord Jesus Christ.

He who began a good work in me will perfect it until the day of Christ Jesus.

I will walk in love and righteousness based on real knowledge and discernment of His glory.

As Christ is proclaimed, I will rejoice.

For me, to live is Christ, to die is gain!

DAY 4
CONCERN FOR OTHERS
Philippians 1:24-26

*24 yet to **remain** on in the flesh is more necessary for your sake.*
    25 And convinced of this, I know that
        *I shall **remain** and **continue** with you all for your **progress** and **joy** in the faith,*
  *26 so that your **proud confidence** in me may abound in Christ Jesus*
       through my coming to you again.

Have you ever been torn between two great opportunities? Perhaps you have been torn between residing close to your family or taking a great job you had been offered.

Paul was torn. He was concerned about his friends. He longed to be in the Presence of God, yet knew that his earthly ministry was not yet complete. It was necessary that he remain with them and continue to guide them in their new Christian faith, as he awaited his personal graduation day. He was *"confident"* that his time was not yet up, although he knew he would face death and, very likely, a violent death.

Paul is telling his friends that his love for them is only matched by his love for the Lord. It is important that both he and they live victoriously and make it to heaven. In verse 25 *"faith"* stands for "experience based on trust in God and on Christ and His redeeming work. For Paul, joy is an indispensable element of that experience."[51]

Paul wanted these Philippians to go forward in their Christian life. He wanted them to do more than progress. He desired them to have fullness of joy. He wanted them to go beyond the original giant leap of faith which resulted in their salvation. He wanted them to move forward, daily, by standing on God's Word.

Love for God is not to be stagnant. Love demands development. From healthy love develops healthy, holy people. Love restricts me from purposefully doing something that will harm another. To be filled with His love we must be filled with Him.[52] "This involves more than a quick stop."[53]

Paul was focused on living a life that honored Christ. Any proud confidence that the Philippians would have in Paul would be because of his and their relationship with Christ, King of kings and Lord of lords!

Good things can come of your "remaining" on this earth. Below are some of the good things that can come from our lives when our focus is on Christ. Read the verses and write out the good that can come.

MATTHEW 22:37-40

_____

_____

2 CORINTHIANS 5:17-21

_____

_____

EXODUS 9:16

_____

_____

GALATIANS 5:22-23

_____

_____

LUKE 6:27

_____

_____

JOHN 13:34

_____

_____

ROMANS 8:28

And we know that God causes all things to work together for good to those who love God, to those who are called according to His purpose.

ROMANS 8:38-39

For I am convinced that neither death, nor life, nor angels, nor principalities, nor things present, nor things to come, nor powers, nor height, nor depth, nor any other created thing, shall be able to separate us from the love of God, which is in Christ Jesus our Lord.

This letter, written so long ago, has become a letter written to us. Paul wants us to live today's destiny in the light of our hope. Paul saw himself, not as a victim, but as a victor: "I'm not chained to them. They are chained to me!" Our world has lost its way and does not know where it's going. We have the answer. **Surrender's Joy** allows us to be light and salt in a desperate world. **Surrender's Joy** only comes, though, if we are surrendered.

MEDITATE

Re-read this devotion and meditate on its implications for your life.

What is the Lord telling you?

_____

_____

_____

_____

_____

_____

_____

MEMORIZE

Review the personalized versions of Philippians 1:2, 6, 9, 18 and 21 below, and repeat them every day.

Grace and peace are mine from God my Father and the Lord Jesus Christ.

He who began a good work in me will perfect it until the day of Christ Jesus.

I will walk in love and righteousness based on real knowledge and discernment of His glory.

As Christ is proclaimed, I will rejoice.

For me, to live is Christ, to die is gain!

DAY 5
WORTHY CONDUCT
Philippians 1:27-30

27 *Only conduct yourselves in a manner worthy of the gospel of Christ;*

   so that whether I come and see you or remain absent,

      I may hear of you that you are

         ***standing firm** in **one** spirit,*

   *with **one mind** striving together for the faith of the gospel;*

      28 *in no way alarmed by your opponents—*

         which is a sign of destruction for them, but of salvation for you, and that too, from God.

            29 *For to you it has been granted for Christ's sake,*

         *not only to **believe** in Him,*

      *but also to **suffer** for His sake,*

   30 *experiencing the same conflict which you saw in me, and now hear to be in me.*

As Christians we are dual citizens. We are *in* the world, but are not to be *of* the world. We live *in* this world, but we are also *in* Christ.

Paul admonishes his friends to "behave as citizens" of a higher realm. They were to walk according to God's principles as revealed in His words.

1. **Stand firm.**

"In the Greek word translated 'stand fast,' the ideas of firmness or uprightness are prominent. It means 'to stand firm and hold one's ground.' The implication is clear that when one holds one's ground, he does it in the face of enemy opposition."[54]

This can also be related to the concept of soldiers standing firm in battle or of believers condemned and fighting for their lives in a Roman amphitheater (Ephesians 6:13; 1 Corinthians 4:9). "To stand firm" could also be expressed negatively as "not to be moved," "not to change" or "not to give up."[55]

It is much easier to stand when we are standing in the power of the Holy Spirit. This requires that our focus remain on Christ as the One who has redeemed us and on the Holy Spirit as the One who empowers us. Our weakness, then, becomes our strength. Our weakness demonstrates our utter need for total dependence on Him!

Summarize some situations or ways God has proven Himself faithful and trustworthy in your life.

_____

_____

_____

_____

_____

LUKE 6:47-49

"Everyone who comes to Me, and hears My words, and acts upon them, I will show you whom he is like: he is like a man building a house, who dug deep and laid a foundation upon the rock; and when a flood rose, the torrent burst against that house and could not shake it, because it had been well built. But the one who has heard, and has not acted accordingly, is like a man who built a house upon the ground without any foundation; and the torrent burst against it and immediately it collapsed, and the ruin of that house was great."

Review the foundation on which you stand by reading the verses below and writing a few words, to the right, to summarize what they say.

EPHESIANS 2:20 –

ROMANS 5:1-2 –

ROMANS 5:3-4 –

ROMANS 5:5 –

ROMANS 15:4 –

ROMANS 15:13 –

1 TIMOTHY 5:5 –

1 TIMOTHY 6:17 –

TITUS 1:2; 2:13; 3:7 –

1 PETER 3:15 –

HEBREWS 6:18-19 –

Now, write out a situation you are currently dealing with and what you need to do differently to stand firm in that situation.

_____

_____

_____

_____

_____

_____

2. Stand firm in **one spirit and one mind.**

Be unified in Christ. Join together in fighting the good fight. Use combined strength.

COLOSSIANS 3:14-17
And beyond all these things put on love, which is the perfect bond of unity. And let the peace of Christ rule in your hearts, to which indeed you were called in one body; and be thankful. Let the word of Christ richly dwell within you, with all wisdom teaching and admonishing one another with psalms and hymns and spiritual songs, singing with thankfulness in your hearts to God. And whatever you do in word or deed, do all in the name of the Lord Jesus, giving thanks through Him to God the Father.

"They are to *'stand fast in one spirit.'* The word *'spirit'* here refers to the unity of spirit in which the members of the church should be fused and blended. The Greek word *'spirit'* is used at times of the disposition or influence which fills and governs the soul of anyone. It is so used here. This unity of spirit when present among the members of a local church, is produced by the Holy Spirit."[56]

"If we could see the divine intention for the church, we would be of one mind. *"One mind"* indicates that we are to be focused on HIS purposes, not our own. When we become Christians, we become members of a battalion that is to be ready for war, not an entertainment corp. The enemy comes against us at the place of our individual weaknesses. There is no weakness in the church when it is united. Where one person is weak, another is strong. Collectively, there is no weakness when there is one mind."[57]

Are you connected to your local Church Body? Why or why not?
What can you do to become more connected?

_____

_____

_____

_____

_____

In what way does connection to the Body help you to stand firm?

_____

_____

_____

_____

_____

3. Stand firm in one spirit and one mind **striving together for the faith of the gospel,** in no way alarmed by your opponents.

You are united by the gospel, so stand together to further the gospel. Keep your focus on Christ so you will not be alarmed by your opponents. They can harm your physical body but cannot steal you from the Father's hand.

> *"Stand* is just that; it involves standing not running. Together, we can stand. It is not God's plan for deliverance to be in isolation. We are to be His Church united. There is no defense for the back of the church. Running exposes us."[58]

Their weapons destroy them. When you stand firm, it is a *"sign of destruction"* to your enemies. (Note: "Sign of destruction" is also translated "Omen of destruction." "Omen" represents a rare Greek word found in the New Testament only here, in Romans 3:25-26 and in 2 Corinthians 8:24. It signifies a proof based on factual evidence, so it is not simply a "foreshadow," but a "sure sign" or "clear omen.")[59]

4. For to you it has been granted for Christ's sake, not only to **believe** in Him, but also to **suffer** for His sake, experiencing the **same conflict** which you saw in me, and now hear to be in me.

Believe

From the Greek word "pisteu," meaning "to believe to the extent of complete trust and reliance."[60]

Suffer

From the Greek word "paschoo," meaning "to undergo an experience, usually difficult, and normally with the implication of physical or psychological suffering."[61]

> *"Today, more than 200 million Christians suffer for their faith, each day threatened with murder and other acts of violence. An additional 350 million Christians are thought to suffer lesser degrees of oppression, including discrimination and restrictions on the practice of their religion."* [62]

Conflict

From "agoon, agoonos," a contest, of athletes, runners, charioteers. Hebrews 12:1 – Any struggle with dangers, annoyances, obstacles, standing in the way of faith, holiness and a desire to spread the gospel: 1 Thessalonians 2:2, Philippians 1:30; 1 Timothy 6:12; 2 Timothy 4:7.[63]

Paul is saying, "Stand firm … for you … have been granted the privilege to believe *AND* suffer. Do not be intimidated by your enemies. Do not shy away from them as a horse does who is startled. Do not be fearful of showing your faith to those who are against you. In the end, you will win and they will lose. God is the primary agent who will give you victory."

MEDITATE

Re-read this devotion and meditate on its implications for your life.

What is the Lord telling you?

_____

_____

_____

_____

_____

_____

_____

MEMORIZE

Memorize the personalized versions of Philippians 1:2, 6, 9, 18, 21 and 27 below, and repeat them every day.

Grace and peace are mine from God my Father and the Lord Jesus Christ.

He who began a good work in me will perfect it until the day of Christ Jesus.

I will walk in love and righteousness based on real knowledge and discernment of His glory.

As Christ is proclaimed, I will rejoice. For me, to live is Christ, to die is gain!

Stand firm in one spirit, with one mind, working to further the gospel.

THE EPISTLE OF PAUL THE APOSTLE
TO THE

PHILIPPIANS.

CHAPTER I.

PAUL and Timotheus, the servants of Jesus Christ, to all the saints in Christ Jesus which are at Philippi, with the bishops and deacons; and peace, from God our Father and from the Lord Jesus Christ.

WEEK THREE
SURRENDER'S HUMILITY

Philippians 2:1-30

Day 1 – Humility's Unity (2:1-4)   57

Day 2 – Humility's Emptying (2:5-8)   63

Day 3 – Humility's Exaltation (2:9-11)   67

Day 4 – Humility's Application (2:12-18)   71

Day 5 – Humility's Examples (2:19-30)   75

UPWARD LIVING IN A WORLD GONE MAD

SURRENDER'S JOY

A Study of Philippians

WEEK THREE

SURRENDER'S HUMILITY

1 *If therefore there is any* **encouragement** *in Christ, if there is any* **consolation** *of love,*
if there is any **fellowship of the Spirit***, if any* **affection and compassion***,*

    2 **make my joy complete** *by being of the* **same mind***,*
      maintaining the **same love***,* **united in spirit***, intent on* **one purpose***.*

    3 *Do nothing from* **selfishness** *or* **empty conceit***,*
    but with **humility of mind** *let each of you* **regard** *one another as more important than himself;*

  4 *do not merely look out for your own personal interests, but also for the interests of others.*

5 *Have* **this attitude** *in yourselves which was also in Christ Jesus,*

    6 *who, although He* **existed** *in the* **form of God***,*
      did not regard equality with God a thing to be **grasped***,*

      7 *but* **emptied Himself***, taking the form of a* **bond-servant***,*
        and being made in the **likeness of men***.*

    8 *And being found in appearance as a man,*
  He **humbled Himself** *by becoming* **obedient** *to the point of death, even death on a cross.*

    9 *Therefore also God highly* **exalted Him***,*
      and **bestowed on Him the name which is above every name***,*

      10 *that at the name of Jesus* **every knee should bow***,*
    of those who are in heaven, and on earth, and under the earth,

    11 *and that* **every tongue should confess** *that* **Jesus Christ is Lord***,*
  to the **glory** *of God the Father.*

12 *So then, my beloved, just as you have always* **obeyed***,*
    not as in my presence only, but now much more in my absence,
      work out your salvation with fear and trembling*;*

    13 *for it is God who is at work in you, both* **to will and to work for His good pleasure***.*

  14 *Do all things without grumbling or disputing;*

15 *that you may prove yourselves to be* **blameless** *and* **innocent***,*
    children of God **above reproach** *in the midst of a crooked and perverse generation,*
      among whom you appear as **lights in the world***,*

16 *holding fast* the word of life, so that in the day of Christ I may have cause to glory
    because I did not run in vain nor toil in vain.

17 But even if I am being poured out as a **drink offering**
    upon the **sacrifice** and **service** of your faith, **I rejoice** and share my joy with you all.

18 And you too, I urge you, rejoice in the same way and share your joy with me.

19 But I hope in the Lord Jesus to send Timothy to you shortly,
    so that I also may be encouraged when I learn of your condition.

20 For I have no one else of kindred spirit
    who will **genuinely be concerned for your welfare**.

21 For they all seek after their own interests, not those of Christ Jesus.

22 But you know of his **proven worth**
    that he **served with me in the furtherance of the gospel like a child serving his father**.

23 Therefore I hope to send him immediately, as soon as I see how things go with me;

24 and I trust in the Lord that I myself also shall be coming shortly.

25 But I thought it necessary to send to you Epaphroditus,
    my brother and fellow worker and fellow soldier,
    who is also your **messenger** and **minister to my need**;

26 because he was longing for you all
    and was distressed because you had heard that he was sick.

27 For indeed he was **sick to the point of death**, but God had mercy on him,
    and not on him only but also on me, lest I should have sorrow upon sorrow.

28 Therefore I have sent him all the more eagerly
    in order that when you see him again you may rejoice and I may be less concerned about you.

29 Therefore **receive him in the Lord** with all joy, and **hold men like him in high regard**;

30 because he came close to death for the work of Christ,
    risking his life to complete what was deficient in your service to me.

DAY 1
HUMILITY'S UNITY
Philippians 2:1-4

1 *If therefore there is any* **encouragement** *in Christ,*
>*if there is any* **consolation** *of love,*
>>*if there is any* **fellowship of the Spirit,**
>>>*if any* **affection and compassion,**
>>**2 make my joy complete**
>>>*by being of the* **same mind,**
>>>>*maintaining the* **same love,**
>>>>>**united in spirit,** *intent on* **one purpose.**
>>**3** *Do nothing from* **selfishness** *or* **empty conceit,**
>*but with* **humility of mind** *let each of you* **regard** *one another as more important than himself;*
4 *do not merely look out for your own personal interests, but also for the interests of others.*

We've often heard the popular slogan, "United we stand. Divided we fall." In regard to the Church, this is a biblical concept that Christians had best heed. **Upward Living** requires that Christians "mind the same thing" that Jesus did. We must do more than *know* better. We must *act* better. We are to stand united as the Church so we can present a united front to the world. The war we are fighting is more than a physical battle. It is a spiritual battle (Ephesians 6:4), and one that will be fought most effectively together!

> *It's one thing for truth to be birthed IN you.*
> *It's another thing for truth to come OUT of you.*
> ~ Des Evans

Apparently there was division in the church, primarily caused by two women, Euodia and Syntyche (4:2). In this chapter, Paul builds on his previous discussion of "unity" by dealing with Christian living. He begins this section with four "if" clauses which are true to fact. These positive statements are used as the sure basis of his appeal in the verses which follow. In other words, "Christ is the *Source* of encouragement, love, fellowship, affection and compassion, so live in a way that is controlled by Him and reflects Him to your brothers and sisters and to the world." **Surrender's Unity** is a good testimony to the world. Let's look more closely at the meaning of some of the key words in the "if" clauses of 2:1-2.

Encouragement

In Greek, "paraklēsis" (n), meaning "a calling to one's side," consolation, exhortation or encouragement.[64]

In Christ

In (en) denotes a fixed position and carries the concept of "your living completely controlled by Christ."[65] You will be encouraged as you live controlled by Christ.

Consolation of love

One could say, "The fact that Christ loves you comforts you." In some languages, a passive expression is used. For example, "you are comforted because Christ loves you." Other languages express "comfort" negatively as "takes away your anxieties," or "causes you not to worry any longer."

Fellowship of the Spirit

Fellowship, in Greek, "koinōnia" (n). This phrase might be expressed as, "you and Christ's Spirit talk together," "you and Christ's Spirit go hand in hand," or "there is a oneness between you and Christ's Spirit."[66]

Affection and compassion

In Greek, "splanchnon" and "oiktirmos." This relates to the feelings and actions of the members of the Philippian church to one another.[67] In view of this, Paul may well have said: (1) Be encouraged and encourage; (2) Be comforted by His love and comfort others, in love; (3) As Christ's Spirit fellowships with you, fellowship with others; and (4) Show affection and compassion to one another.

Paul has no doubt, whatsoever, that the four "if" clauses (2:1) are realities in the experience of the Philippian Christians. But this knowledge is not enough to make his heart sing with joy, for it is overshadowed by the petty jealousies he has heard about among the members.

"Make my joy complete" or "complete my joy." "Complete":

Revelation 6:11 – To make it complete in every detail.

Luke 7:1 – To bring to realization.

Romans 13:8 – To accomplish.

Matthew 1:22 – To fulfill.[68]

Read verses 2-4 again. What would make Paul's joy complete?

_____

_____

_____

Here, Paul urges the members to stay focused on their God-given purpose (2:2). As a member of the Body, they were part of something bigger than their own petty differences. In view of this, Paul admonishes them to:

1) Be of the *"same mind,"* be "minding the same" or think the way Jesus did.

    ROMANS 12:16-18
    Be of the same mind toward one another; do not be haughty in mind, but associate with the lowly. Do not be wise in your own estimation. Never pay back evil for evil to anyone. Respect what is right in the sight of all men.

2) Maintain the *"same love"* or love as God loved (agape love).

    1 PETER 3:8-9
    To sum up, let all be harmonious, sympathetic, brotherly, kindhearted, and humble in spirit; not returning evil for evil, or insult for insult, but giving a blessing instead; for you were called for the very purpose that you might inherit a blessing."

3) *"United (fellow-souled) in spirit"* (one accord), instead of focused on your own desires.

    PSALM 133:1
    Behold, how good and how pleasant it is for brothers to dwell together in unity!

4) *"Intent on one purpose."*

    LUKE 4:43
    But He said to them, "I must preach the kingdom of God to the other cities also, for I was sent for this purpose."

    EPHESIANS 1:10-12
    In Him also we have obtained an inheritance, having been predestined according to His purpose who works all things after the counsel of His will, to the end that we who were the first to hope in Christ should be to the praise of His glory.

1 TIMOTHY 4:7-8

But have nothing to do with worldly fables fit only for old women. On the other hand, discipline yourself for the purpose of godliness; for bodily discipline is only of little profit, but godliness is profitable for all things, since it holds promise for the present life and also for the life to come.

1 PETER 4:6

For the gospel has for this purpose been preached even to those who are dead, that though they are judged in the flesh as men, they may live in the spirit according to the will of God.

1 PETER 4:7-8

The end of all things is at hand; therefore, be of sound judgment and sober spirit for the purpose of prayer.

"Paul had prayed a prayer of supplication for them. He saw beyond the obvious to what God had in mind for them … their destiny. He could see the signs of increased future persecution. They could only see what was right in front of them. They had to learn to live beyond the ordinary. It is one thing to do something once in a while, and act like that is where you live. It's another to live there all the time. To embrace grace, we must also embrace our weakness and to allow His strength to make us more than we can be in ourselves. When we are surrendered, the purposes of God cause an updraft!"[69]

Positionally, we are complete in Him and have the righteousness of God in Christ. Practically, sometimes we hit it and sometimes we don't. If we aim too low it leads to mediocrity instead of excellence. God is asking us to not settle for mediocrity, but to go beyond the norm. He has called us to be *in* the world but not *of* it. We are not to be changed by the world but to change it. We are to be different, to reflect Christ. God in us empowers us to live our daily destiny.

Christ is so much more than we can imagine, while the object of romantic love ends up being so much less than we imagine. What joy there is in daily surrendering every area of our lives to the One who is so much more! We, then, allow Him to make us so much more than we can otherwise be! The result is that He is able to use us in ways beyond our natural weaknesses.

Paul wanted the Philippians to move closer to perfection, so that the purposes of God and practices of their lives would be harmonious. He wanted them to glory in things that had value instead of allowing the tyranny of self to seek those things that had no worth or value.

What is of lasting value? List some things that are of value.

_____

_____

_____

List some things that have only passing value.

_____

_____

_____

What priority do the most valuable things have in your life? If Paul were alive today, would his review of your life make his joy complete? Why or why not?

_____

_____

_____

Is there any area that you have attitudes or actions that are selfish or based on empty conceit? Are you focused on His purpose, reflecting His love?

_____

_____

_____

Pray and allow the Lord to reveal to you attitudes, habits and actions that need to change. List these things below. Choose to consciously change one thing immediately.

_____

_____

_____

_____

_____

_____

_____

_____

MEDITATE

Re-read this devotion and meditate on its implications for your life.

What is the Lord telling you?

_____

_____

_____

_____

_____

_____

_____

MEMORIZE

Memorize the personalized versions of Philippians 1:2, 6, 9, 18, 21, 27 and 2:4 below, and repeat them every day.

Grace and peace are mine from God my Father and the Lord Jesus Christ.

He who began a good work in me will perfect it until the day of Christ Jesus.

I will walk in love and righteousness based on real knowledge and discernment of His glory.

As Christ is proclaimed, I will rejoice. For me, to live is Christ, to die is gain!

I will stand firm in one spirit, with one mind, working to further the gospel, thinking of others as more important than myself.

DAY 2
HUMILITY'S EMPTYING
Philippians 2:5-8

5 *Have **this attitude** in yourselves which was also in Christ Jesus,*

    6 *who, although He **existed** in the **form of God**,*

        *did not regard equality with God a thing to be **grasped**,*

            7 *but **emptied Himself**,*

        *taking the form of a **bond-servant**,*

      *and being made in the **likeness of men**.*

8 *And being found in appearance as a man,*

    *He **humbled Himself** by becoming **obedient** to the point of death,*

      even death on a cross.

I have a hard time wrapping my mind around the amazing fact of the incarnation … God became flesh and dwelt among us. I admit it, sometimes I become dismayed at the behavior of some who represent themselves as Christians. But every time I look at Jesus directly, I only see incredible beauty. In these verses, there is mind-numbing brilliance and intensity. Paul wants us to take more than a superficial look at Him. He doesn't want us to look away.

Jesus did not have to grasp at being God. He was and is fully God. Over and over other scriptures proclaim this fact. Here are just two of them: *"In the beginning was the Word, and the Word was with God, and the Word was God"* (John 1:1). *"And He is the image of the invisible God, the first-born of all creation"* (Colossians 1:15-16).

As God, Jesus is worshiped in heaven.

REVELATION 5:11-14
And I looked, and I heard the voice of many angels around the throne and the living creatures and the elders; and the number of them was myriads of myriads, and thousands of thousands, saying with a loud voice, "Worthy is the Lamb that was slain to receive power and riches and wisdom and might and honor and glory and blessing."

And every created thing which is in heaven and on the earth and under the earth and on the sea, and all things in them, I heard saying, "To Him who sits on the throne, and to the Lamb, be blessing and honor and glory and dominion forever and ever."

And the four living creatures kept saying, "Amen." And the elders fell down and worshiped.

When Jesus became man, He did not set aside His God-essence. Jesus' unchangeable, inner essence (*"form,"* from the Greek word *"morphe"*) was divine. He was God. "His outward form *"schema"* did change, but He remained in His being, God. He was God when He was born in Bethlehem. He was God when He was 8, 18 and 28. He was God when He died and when He arose from the grave."[70] "When we come to consider the fact that our Lord laid aside something, we will see that it was not the *possession* but the *expression* of the divine essence."[71]

Unbelievable as it seems, the Son of God emptied Himself (v. 7) or made Himself of no reputation. Willingly, Jesus took off His brilliant sparkling prestigious crown and took on the weakness of human flesh (a *"bond servant"*) and the humiliation of the lowest form of death. On the other hand, our own crowns are attached to our heads with cement! If we want to see man at his best, we have to look at Jesus.

JOHN 10:18
"No one has taken it away from Me, but I lay it down on My own initiative. I have authority to lay it down, and I have authority to take it up again. This commandment I received from My Father."

The desire to serve others would always have been part of His nature as Diety. When He took on the form of a bondslave who came to serve, though, He traded one form of expression for another.

In the Roman society, people never fought to be last. The same is true today. Jesus, God in the flesh, had every right to proclaim His number one position. Instead, He willingly became last, taking on the form of decaying flesh.

Sadly, people often let go of priceless treasure for a moment's pleasure. God became a part of humanity that humanity might be raised to a higher level. "Let this mind be in you …." Why? Because it usually isn't. Only in the Spirit can we see that we are people of two worlds and keep the proper perspective.

If death on a cross was humiliating to our Lord in His humanity, how much more was it in His deity? Christ's likeness to man was a real likeness. As a man, Christ was obedient. As men and women, we can also walk in obedience. "Have this attitude in yourselves."

Contrast the difference between Jesus' attitude and actions with the world's philosophy in the chart below.

JESUS' ATTITUDES AND ACTIONS PHILIPPIANS 2:5-11	THE WORLD'S PHILOSOPHY AND HOW THAT AFFECTS INDIVIDUAL'S ATTITUDES AND ACTIONS ROMANS 1:18-28

When we walk in the light of Jesus' example, how does it transform our thinking and actions?

_____

_____

_____

_____

Read 2 Corinthians 8:9. How do we become rich through His poverty?

_____

_____

_____

We must note that Jesus became obedient to the point of death, but not just any crises of death, it was an excruciating, torturous, cruel death on the cross. It was the death of a common criminal.

MEDITATE

Re-read this devotion and meditate on its implications for your life.

What is the Lord telling you?

_____

_____

_____

_____

_____

_____

MEMORIZE

Memorize the personalized versions of Philippians 1:2, 6, 9, 18, 21, 27 and 2:4-5 below, and repeat them every day.

Grace and peace are mine from God my Father and the Lord Jesus Christ.

He who began a good work in me will perfect it until the day of Christ Jesus.

I will walk in love and righteousness based on real knowledge and discernment of His glory.

As Christ is proclaimed, I will rejoice. For me, to live is Christ, to die is gain!

I will stand firm in one spirit, with one mind, working to further the gospel, thinking of others as more important than myself, having Christ's servant attitude.

DAY 3
HUMILITY'S EXALTATION
Philippians 2:9-11

9 *Therefore also God highly* **exalted Him,**

and **bestowed on Him the name which is above every name,**

10 *that at the name of Jesus* **every knee should bow,**

of those who are in heaven, and on earth, and under the earth,

11 *and that* **every tongue should confess** *that* **Jesus Christ is Lord,**

to the **glory** *of God the Father.*

His Presence is unnerving.

In the light of that Presence, the prophet Isaiah proclaimed, *"Woe is me, for I am ruined! Because I am a man of unclean lips, and I live among a people of unclean lips; for my eyes have seen the King, the Lord of hosts"* (Isaiah 6:11).

As he meditated on God's greatness and power, David sang,

> O Lord, our Lord,
> How majestic is Your name in all the earth,
> Who have displayed Your splendor above the heavens!
> From the mouth of infants and nursing babes You have established strength
> Because of Your adversaries,
> To make the enemy and the revengeful cease.
> When I consider Your heavens, the work of Your fingers,
> The moon and the stars, which You have ordained;
> What is man that You take thought of him,
> And the son of man that You care for him?
> Yet You have made him a little lower than God,
> And You crown him with glory and majesty!
> You make him to rule over the works of Your hands;
> You have put all things under his feet,
> All sheep and oxen,
> And also the beasts of the field,
> The birds of the heavens and the fish of the sea,
> Whatever passes through the paths of the seas.
> O Lord, our Lord,
> How majestic is Your name in all the earth! (Psalm 8:1-9)

Jesus was and is fully God. He was a member of the "us" who made the world and mankind: *Then God said, "Let Us make man in Our image, according to Our likeness"* (Genesis 1:26). And, He is God who laid down status symbols of His glory, took the form of a servant and died for our sins.

In the kingdom of God, exaltation is the natural result of humiliation. Philippians 2:9-11 describe the restoration of that original glory and the bestowing of additional honor.

Upon Jesus was bestowed not "a" name, but "the" Name.

The definite article appears in the Greek text and refers to a particular name. The title, THE NAME, is a very common Hebrew title, denoting office, rank, dignity. The expression, "The Name of God" in the Old Testament, denotes the divine Presence, the divine Majesty, especially as the object of adoration and praise. The context here dwells upon the honor and worship bestowed on Him upon whom this name was conferred. The conferring of this title "The Name," was upon the Lord Jesus as the Son of Man. A Man, the Man Christ Jesus, who as Very God had voluntarily laid aside His expression of the glory of Deity during His incarnation, now has placed upon His shoulders all the majesty, dignity and glory of Deity itself. It is the God-Man who stooped to the depths of humiliation, who is raised, not as God now, although He was all that, but as Man, to the infinite height of exaltation possessed only by Deity. It is the answer of our Lord's prayer: "And now, O Father, glorify thou Me with Thine own self with the glory which I had with Thee before the world was" (John 17:5 KJV). It is the glory of Deity, not now seen shining in infinite splendor as in His pre-incarnate state, but that glory shining in perfect contrast to and with His glorified humanity raised now to a place of equal dignity with Deity. It is the ideal and beautiful combination of the exaltation of Deity and the humility of Deity seen in incarnate Deity.[72]

"Highly exalted" (2:9) *"huperupsoosen."* First aorist indicative of huperupsoo huper and hupsos a late and rare word (Septuagint and Byzantine). Only used here in the New Testament. Because of Christ's voluntary humiliation, God lifted Him above or beyond "huper," the state of glory which He enjoyed before He took on the form of Man. What glory did Christ have after the Ascension that He did not have before in heaven? What did He take back to heaven that He did not bring? Clearly His humanity. He returned to heaven the Son of Man as well as the Son of God."[73]

"The qualifications of the Saviour of the World were so extraordinary, the redeeming acts so stupendous, and the result of all so glorious both to God and man, that it is impossible to conceive a higher name or title than that of JESUS, Savior of the World."[74]

In view of His highly exalted position of divinity, it is natural that all in heaven, on earth and things under the earth should worship Him, and honor Him as being the universal sovereign Lord (2:10). Here, we must draw attention to the clear difference between heartfelt high worship that is cheerful and freely offered and the constrained worship of those who feel forced to acknowledge His authority.

REVELATION 5:13-14

And every created thing which is in heaven and on the earth and under the earth and on the sea, and all things in them, I heard saying, "To Him who sits on the throne, and to the Lamb, be blessing and honor and glory and dominion forever and ever." And the four living creatures kept saying, "Amen." And the elders fell down and worshiped.

In all that Christ is and does on a daily basis, God's glory shows. Jesus became like us that we might be raised to a higher level. Take a leap of faith and let Him raise you to a new place!

> *"God will not take us where the peace of God will not keep us."*
> ~ *Unknown Author*

The Lord who is over all, wants to be over you.

The Lord who is enough, wants to be enough for you.

Jesus is more than the God-Man who walked upon the water, healed the sick, taught the multitudes and raised the dead. **He wants to be more than exalted on high. He wants to be exalted in you!**

Surrender to Christ's Lordship is a day-by-day, minute-by-minute endeavor. It is an acknowledgement of His glory. Write out a prayer of surrender below.

_____

_____

_____

_____

_____

_____

_____

_____

MEDITATE

Re-read this devotion and meditate on its implications for your life.

What is the Lord telling you?

_____

_____

_____

_____

_____

_____

_____

MEMORIZE

Memorize the personalized versions of Philippians 1:2, 6, 9, 18, 21, 27, 2:4-5 and 11 below, and repeat them every day.

Grace and peace are mine from God my Father and the Lord Jesus Christ.

He who began a good work in me will perfect it until the day of Christ Jesus.

I will walk in love and righteousness based on real knowledge and discernment of His glory.

As Christ is proclaimed, I will rejoice. For me, to live is Christ, to die is gain!

I will stand firm in one spirit, with one mind, working to further the gospel, thinking of others as more important than myself, having Christ's servant attitude.

That every tongue should confess that Jesus Christ is Lord, to the glory of God the Father.

DAY 4
HUMILITY'S APPLICATION
Philippians 2:12-18

12 *So then, my beloved, just as you have always* **obeyed**,
not as in my presence only,
but now much more in my absence,
work out your salvation with fear and trembling;
13 *for it is God who is at work in you,*
both **to will and to work for His good pleasure**.
14 *Do all things without grumbling or disputing;*
15 *that you may prove yourselves to be* **blameless** *and* **innocent**,
children of God **above reproach**
in the midst of a crooked and perverse generation,
among whom you appear as **lights in the world**,
16 **holding fast** *the word of life,*
so that in the day of Christ I may have cause to glory
because I did not run in vain nor toil in vain.
17 *But even if I am being poured out as a* **drink offering**
upon the **sacrifice** *and* **service** *of your faith,*
I rejoice and share my joy with you all.
18 *And you too, I urge you,*
rejoice in the same way and **share your joy** *with me.*

Paul wanted his deeply beloved disciples to be at peace over him, and he wanted to be at peace over them. They held a special place in his heart, and he couldn't keep them out of his mind. Paul had witnessed the faithful past obedience of his disciples at Philippi. During his separation from them, though, he had grown anxious over the lack of knowledge. Now Epaphroditus was with him, bringing gifts and encouragement. Unfortunately, he also brought word of some "grumbling and disputing" that had arisen between some of the members. The Apostle wanted this dear body of people to live upward without a negative outward expression. As Christians, they were to have the servant attitude Christ had and obey as He obeyed (v. 12).

"Work out" carries with it the sense of "fully give all your strength to" the task until it is finished. In other words, "Don't get sidetracked and settle for second best. Represent Christ well. Finish the course. Go for the goal of the high calling!"

In this context, "salvation" seems to relate, mainly, to the living of a life well-pleasing to the Lord[75] and to the health and spiritual well-being of the Christian community. It could be interpreted as, "cause your well-being to be complete." The Philippians are urged to work toward this goal with caution *("fear and trembling")* or humble reverence, dependence and complete devotion to God (see Psalm 2:11; Isaiah 19:16).

"For it is God who is at work in you, both to will and to work for His good pleasure" (v. 13). If you are allowing God to work in you, you will cooperate with Him by working yourself to restore the spiritual welfare of your own church community; otherwise, you will be actually impeding His work! A Christian who is walking in obedience will be allowing God's Spirit to bring forth His fruit in their lives (love, joy, peace, long-suffering, gentleness, self-control). They will not be unforgiving and will put aside their own selfish desires.

"Do all things without grumbling (gongýzō) or disputing; that you may prove yourselves to be blameless and innocent" (v. 14-15). This seems to infer that you can only be blameless and innocent IF you do all things without grumbling or disputing (arguing)! It seems as if complaining brings blame upon the complainer! Think about it.

The chief root word used means "to murmur" and is the same word used in regard to the complaining by the Israelites as they wondered in the wilderness: murmurs against Moses (Exodus 15:24), Moses and Aaron (Exodus 16:2) and God (Exodus 16:7-8). There are always grounds for grumbling. For example, the lack of water. The foul attitude and murmuring is called the tempting (Exodus 17:2) or scorning (Numbers 14:11) of God.[76]

It was this murmuring and discontent that kept the Israelites on their endless journey through the wilderness and hindered them from entering the Promised Land. It would be the murmuring and argumentative spirit ("disputing") of the Philippians against each other that would mutilate the vision of Christ they reflected to the world.

(Note: "Disputing" would seem to relate more to being argumentative. It is not to be related to analyzing or questioning the truth, practicality or logic of a situation, statement or action.)

Paul urges Christians to, *"Prove yourselves to be blameless and innocent children of God above reproach"* (v. 15). He knew the world was ugly and dark and did not want Christians to be contaminated by the world's self-serving, "crooked and perverse" philosophy.

"In order for us to be the soldiers Christ wants us to be, truth must be birthed in us, and it must come out of us! God expects us to do more than 'know better'—we are to act better!"[77]

Christians are to mirror the attitudes and actions of Christ. We are to shine as pure gold, undefiled by foreign mixtures.

There are many foreign mixtures that can defile a Christian. Two that I can think of are lack of forgiveness and selfishness. Are you bitter toward someone? Are any of your actions self-serving? It's time to forgive. It's time to surrender.

Are there any other foreign mixtures that are defiling you? What are they? List them and then lay them at the cross and allow His blood to cleanse you and His power to strengthen you.

_____

_____

_____

_____

_____

_____

Re-read verses 12-19.

Christians are to appear as lights to the world, as we hold fast/forth *(epechō)* the Word of life. According to various Bible translators, language experts and commentators, there is the sense in verse 16 both of *holding firmly* on to the Word of life, *holding toward* the Word of life and *holding forth* the Word of life. We are to both hold firmly on to the truth and promises of His Word and to offer them as a gift to those we meet. As we *"hold fast"* to Him, we are illuminated by His light and will be able to reflect His light to the world.

In verse 16, Paul appears to be picturing himself as looking back on his life from the beginning of his work to his end at the finish line. Paul sacrificed his life as a "drink offering" on the behalf of those he served. In general, he lived his life for others, not for himself. His life had been poured out as an offering to the Philippians and others, for the benefit of their faith in God and His purpose. He tells them, "As you hold on to, act according to and offer the message that causes people to really live, I will have reason to be proud of you. I will know that I did not work hard for nothing."

Are there any behaviors in your life that might actually be impeding His work in your family, church and in the world? List them below. Now that they are out in the open, intentionally seek to change them by allowing His Spirit to work in your life and by using self-control.

_____

_____

_____

_____

_____

_____

MEDITATE

Re-read this devotion and meditate on its implications for your life.

What is the Lord telling you?

_____

_____

_____

_____

_____

_____

MEMORIZE

Memorize the personalized versions of Philippians 1:2, 6, 9, 18, 21, 27, 2:4-5, 11 and 14 below, and repeat them every day.

Grace and peace are mine from God my Father and the Lord Jesus Christ.

He who began a good work in me will perfect it until the day of Christ Jesus.

I will walk in love and righteousness based on real knowledge and discernment of His glory.

As Christ is proclaimed, I will rejoice. For me, to live is Christ, to die is gain!

I will stand firm in one spirit, with one mind, working to further the gospel, thinking of others as more important than myself, having Christ's servant attitude.

That every tongue should confess that Jesus Christ is Lord, to the glory of God the Father.

I will do all without grumbling or disputing.

DAY 5
HUMILITY'S EXAMPLES
Philippians 2:19-30

19 *But I hope in the Lord Jesus to send Timothy to you shortly,*

   so that I also may be encouraged when I learn of your condition.

   20 *For I have no one else of kindred spirit*

   *who will **genuinely be concerned for your welfare**.*

   21 *For they all seek after their own interests,*

   not those of Christ Jesus.

   22 *But you know of his **proven worth***

   *that **he served with me in the furtherance of the gospel***

   ***like a child serving his father**.*

   23 *Therefore I hope to send him immediately,*

   as soon as I see how things go with me;

   24 *and I trust in the Lord that I myself also shall be coming shortly.*

25 *But I thought it necessary to send to you Epaphroditus,*

my brother and fellow worker and fellow soldier,

*who is also your **messenger** and **minister to my need**;*

   26 *because **he was longing for you all***

   and was distressed because you had heard that he was sick.

   27 *For indeed he was **sick to the point of death**,*

but God had mercy on him, and not on him only but also on me,

lest I should have sorrow upon sorrow.

28 *Therefore I have sent him all the more eagerly*

in order that when you see him again you may rejoice

and I may be less concerned about you.

   29 *Therefore **receive him in the Lord***

   *with all joy, and **hold men like him in high regard**;*

   30 *because he came close to death for the work of Christ,*

***risking his life to complete what was deficient in your service to me**.*

Now Paul takes some time to commend two faithful men who are godly examples of the positive characteristics he has been encouraging the Philippians to emulate in 1:3-2:18. The first one is Timothy, whom he describes as his "own son in the faith" (Acts 16:3), and the second is Epaphroditus, a Philippian, who almost died bringing a much needed gift to Paul.

Timothy

Timothy was fairly young when he first met the apostle Paul. His father was a Greek Gentile. His mother was Jewish. Timothy is first mentioned in the Bible during Paul's second visit to Lystra (Acts 16:1-2). He had been recommended by several congregations. Paul, impressed by this young "disciple," described him as his "own son in the faith." He even arranged for Timothy to become his ministry and traveling companion (Acts 16:3; 18:5), and personally circumcised him so he might be accepted by both Jews and Gentiles.

Paul speaks highly of both Eunice and Lois when he writes to Timothy: *"I thank God, whom I serve with a clear conscience the way my forefathers did, as I constantly remember you in my prayers night and day, longing to see you, even as I recall your tears, so that I may be filled with joy. For I am mindful of the sincere faith within you, which first dwelt in your grandmother Lois, and your mother Eunice, and I am sure that it is in you as well"* (2 Timothy 1:3-5).

There is some indication that Timothy was naturally timid (2 Timothy 1:6-8), yet he is also described as one who was strong in the faith (v. 5). Certainly he proved himself as one who could stand strong in the face of persecution. He was one who had courageously presented the gospel. His faith in God made him strong.

Timothy became a dear friend to Paul. He faithfully served the Apostle, even while he was behind bars. On more than one occasion, Timothy almost died. Right before Paul died, in 67 AD, he used his "last words" (2 Timothy) to express concern for the churches and specifically for Timothy. With those words, he encouraged Timothy, and all other believers, to persevere in faith.

Timothy is praised by Paul for his knowledge of the Scriptures and was, at one point, urged by Paul to oversee the church in Ephesus, in Asia Minor (around 65 AD). Tradition indicates he served there for 15 years until he was stoned to death by angry pagans as he preached the gospel.[78]

Read verses 19-22 and summarize the positive things Paul writes about Timothy. Why is Timothy's example especially important in light of the topics Paul has been discussing in the previous verses?

_____

_____

_____

_____

Paul tells the Philippians that he will send Timothy to them after his letter has been delivered by Epaphroditus. He knew that they would be encouraged by Timothy, and he would be encouraged to know that they had followed the directives in his letter.

In Paul's eyes, no one is on the same level as his longtime faithful companion and friend (v. 20): *"For I have no one else of kindred spirit who will genuinely be concerned for your welfare."* *"Kindred spirit"* is really one word in Greek—literally "equal-souled." The term is rare and means to be in complete agreement with someone in the context of a personal relationship.[79]

What does the word *"genuinely"* communicate about the type of concern Timothy has for the Philippians' welfare? List some words that are the opposite of genuine.

_____

_____

_____

What does the statement, *"For they all seek after their own interests, not those of Christ Jesus"* (v. 21), have to do with surrender? Does seeking after your own interests lead to joy? Why or why not?

_____

_____

_____

_____

What does a careful reading of verses 25-29 reveal to you about Epaphroditus?

_____

_____

_____

Epaphroditus

Epaphroditus was a messenger from the Philippian Church, sent to minister to Paul. As a minister, he was functioning officially on their behalf, offering to Paul, *"an acceptable sacrifice, pleasing to God"* (Philippians 4:18). Paul shows his high regard for Epaphroditus with five different descriptive names:

> (1) my **brother**;
>
> (2) my **coworker**;
>
> (3) my **fellow-soldier**;
>
> (4) your **messenger**;
>
> (5) your **minister**.

In this context, the term *"brother"* relates to Epaphroditus' relationship to Paul in the Lord. He and Paul shared a common heritage. They belonged to the same family. There was a bonding of grace. *"Brother"* also communicates the warm personal intimacy and friendship they enjoyed. In the midst of a difficulty they would fight together, as brothers.

"Coworker" occurs 13 times in the New Testament. In all but one case it refers to a commitment to the furtherance of the gospel and the work associated with that mission. Epaphroditus had a track record of being a laborer, not a loiterer. He did not view his trip as a vacation. As soon as he arrived, and was well, he began to work. He had represented his church family well. He didn't forget the reason he was there—to minister to Paul on their behalf. In our actions, we also must not forget we are representing our family.

My *"fellow-soldier"* carries the idea of one who has fought the battles and endured the hardship connected to the preaching of the gospel and ministering to people. Epaphroditus had done more than just "play soldier," he had been in real battles. He had the will and strength to go on to fight future battles, in Christ.

What type of battle had Epaphroditus fought in carrying out the ministry task he had been sent to do? See verses 27 and 30.

_____

_____

_____

_____

Why was Epaphroditus distressed?

_____

_____

_____

(Note: Epaphroditus may have also been distressed out of concern that the Philippians might have thought that he had not carried out his mission well and had, perhaps, been a burden to Paul.)

What purpose does Paul indicate in sending Epaphroditus to them? See verse 28.

_____

_____

_____

Remember some of our earlier discussion relating to the discord in the Philippian church. How could the delivery of this letter help him to be free from anxiety?

_____

_____

_____

Why does Paul tell the Philippians to *"hold men like him in high regard?"* Read verses 29-30.

_____

_____

_____

What character quality does Epaphroditus' actions show? How does this relate to surrender?

_____

_____

_____

Paul urged the Philippians to receive Epaphroditus with ALL joy. They were to hold nothing back in their high regard. As a messenger, he had done an excellent job, almost to the point of losing his life. He took enormous risks and set aside his own personal safety to serve another.

Right before his death, Paul proclaimed, *"For I am already being poured out as a drink offering, and the time of my departure has come. I have fought the good fight, I have finished the course, I have kept the faith; in the future there is laid up for me the crown of righteousness, which the Lord, the righteous Judge, will award to me on that day; and not only to me, but also to all who have loved His appearing"* (2 Timothy 4:5-8).

Do you think Timothy and Epaphroditus were able to make a similar proclamation?

Will you be able to make this proclamation? Is this part of **Surrender's Joy**?

MEDITATE

Re-read this devotion and meditate on its implications for your life.

What is the Lord telling you?

_____

_____

_____

_____

_____

_____

_____

MEMORIZE

Memorize the personalized versions of Philippians 1:2, 6, 9, 18, 21, 27, 2:4-5, 11, 14 and 16 below, and repeat them every day.

Grace and peace are mine from God my Father and the Lord Jesus Christ.

He who began a good work in me will perfect it until the day of Christ Jesus.

I will walk in love and righteousness based on real knowledge and discernment of His glory.

As Christ is proclaimed, I will rejoice. For me, to live is Christ, to die is gain!

I will stand firm in one spirit, with one mind, working to further the gospel, thinking of others as more important than myself, having Christ's servant attitude.

That every tongue should confess that Jesus Christ is Lord, to the glory of God the Father.

I will do all without grumbling or disputing, holding fast and holding forth the Word of life.

WEEK FOUR
SURRENDER'S REJOICING

Philippians 3:1-21

Day 1 – Rejoicing's Confidence (3:1-9)   87

Day 2 – Rejoicing's Righteousness (3:4-10)   92

Day 3 – Rejoicing's Focus (3:11-16)   96

Day 4 – Rejoicing's Pattern (3:15-19)   100

Day 5 – Rejoicing's Citizenship (3:20-21)   104

UPWARD LIVING IN A WORLD GONE MAD
SURRENDER'S JOY
A Study of Philippians

WEEK FOUR

SURRENDER'S REJOICING

1 *Finally, my brethren, **rejoice in the Lord**.*

    (To write the same things again is no trouble to me,

        and it is a safeguard for you.)

        2 *Beware of the dogs,*

            *beware of the **evil workers**,*

                *beware of the **false circumcision**;*

                    3 *for we are the **true circumcision**, who **worship in the Spirit of God***

        *and **glory in Christ Jesus** and put **no confidence** in the **flesh**,*

    4 *although I myself might have confidence even in the flesh.*

If anyone else has a mind to put confidence in the flesh, I far more:

    5 *circumcised the eighth day, of the nation of Israel,*

        of the tribe of Benjamin, a Hebrew of Hebrews;

            as to the Law, a Pharisee;

                6 *as to zeal, a persecutor of the church;*

        as to the righteousness which is in the Law, found blameless.

    7 *But whatever things were **gain** to me,*

        *those things I have **counted as loss** for the sake of Christ.*

        8 *More than that, **I count all things to be loss***

            *in view of the **surpassing value** of knowing Christ Jesus my Lord,*

                *for whom **I have suffered the loss of all things**,*

                    *and count them but **rubbish** in order that I may gain Christ,*

            9 *and may be found in Him,*

        not having a righteousness of my own derived from the Law,

    but that which is through faith in Christ,

  *the **righteousness** which comes from God on the **basis of faith**,*

    10 *that I may **know** Him, and the **power of His resurrection***

*and the **fellowship of His sufferings**, being **conformed** to His death;*

11 *in order that I may attain to the resurrection from the dead.*

12 *Not that I have already obtained it,*

    or have already become perfect,

        *but **I press on***

        in order that I may lay hold of that for which also I was laid hold of by Christ Jesus.

    13 *Brethren, I do not regard myself as having laid hold of it yet;*

but one thing I do:

forgetting what lies behind

    *and **reaching forward** to what lies ahead,*

      14 ***I press on** toward the goal for the **prize** of the **upward call** of God in Christ Jesus.*

        15 *Let us therefore, as many as are **perfect**,*

          *have **this attitude**;*

            *and if in anything you have a **different** attitude,*

        God will reveal that also to you;

    16 *however, let us keep living by that **same standard to which we have attained**.*

      17 *Brethren, join in following **my example**,*

        *and observe those who walk according to the **pattern** you have in us.*

        18 *For many walk, of whom I often told you,*

        *and now tell you even weeping, that they are **enemies of the cross** of Christ,*

      19 *whose **end is destruction**, whose **god is their appetite**,*

    *and whose **glory is in their shame**,*

*who **set their minds on earthly things**.*

20 *For our **citizenship** is in heaven,*

    from which also we eagerly wait for a Savior, the Lord Jesus Christ;

      21 *who will **transform** the body of our humble state*

        *into **conformity** with the body of **His glory**,*

          *by the **exertion of the power** that He has*

        *even to **subject all things to Himself**.*

DAY 1
REJOICING'S CONFIDENCE
Philippians 3:1-9

1 *Finally, my brethren, **rejoice in the Lord**.*

    (To write the same things again is no trouble to me, and it is a safeguard for you.)

        *2 Beware of the dogs, beware of the **evil workers**, beware of the **false circumcision**;*

    *3 for we are the **true circumcision**,*

        *who **worship in the Spirit of God***

            *and **glory in Christ Jesus***

        *and put **no confidence** in the **flesh**,*

4 *although I myself might have confidence even in the flesh.*

    If anyone else has a mind to put confidence in the flesh, I far more:

        5 circumcised the eighth day,

            of the nation of Israel,

                of the tribe of Benjamin,

                    a Hebrew of Hebrews;

                        as to the Law, a Pharisee;

        6 as to zeal, a persecutor of the church;

        as to the righteousness which is in the Law, found blameless.

        *7 But whatever things were **gain** to me,*

    *those things I have **counted as loss** for the sake of Christ.*

8 *More than that, **I count all things to be loss***

    *in view of the **surpassing value** of knowing Christ Jesus my Lord,*

        *for whom **I have suffered the loss of all things**,*

            *and count them but **rubbish** in order that I may gain Christ,*

        9 and may be found in Him,

        not having a righteousness of my own derived from the Law,

    but that which is through faith in Christ,

    *the **righteousness** which comes from God on the **basis of faith**,*

"Through the genius of the Holy Spirit, this letter has transcended the time in which it was written and has become a personal letter to us."[80] In his imprisoned state, Paul is urging us, for the fifth time, to, *"rejoice in the Lord"* (3:1)! Do you get the impression that he really wants us to get it? In total, Paul uses "rejoice" or "joy" 19 times in this letter.

God wants us to take our eyes off the horizontal difficulties and put them on Him. Has He saved us and kept us? **Then, rejoice in the Lord!** Has He walked alongside us through the difficulties and made a way where there seemed no way? **Then, rejoice in the Lord!** "But, things aren't going as planned." Whose plan are you talking about? God knows what is ahead and He knows what we need to learn to get through. **So, rejoice in the Lord!**

Rejoice that you are His. When you are in Him, you have so much going for you. When trouble comes, He will either take you through it, around it or release you from it. Rejoice. You cannot base your sense of well-being on what is around you. That will only lead to discouragement and disillusionment. Rejoice that He is in you and always with you. *It is easier to deal with difficult situations if you have inner peace and are keeping your eyes on Him.*

Under Nero, the church was getting ready to go through the most intense persecution they had yet experienced. They would have to walk in **Surrender's Rejoicing** to make it through.

Paul goes on to say, *"To write the same things again is no trouble to me, and it is a safeguard for you."*

What does the word "safeguard" communicate to you?

_____

_____

_____

Safeguard

    pertaining to a state of safety and security, and hence free from danger – safe, safely, secure, securely.[81]

The fact that Paul was providing them with a written record was a safeguard because it was something they could refer back to. The content of the letter was a safeguard because it would help them to continue to grow in their faith, deal with church issues, encourage them and prepare them for what was ahead. Maintaining Christ-focus would be a safeguard for their minds.

Review chapters one and two. Comment, below, on some of the topics Paul dealt with and how they serve as a safeguard.

_____

_____

_____

_____

_____

Paul goes on to warn his friends (v. 2) of those Judaizing teachers (called "dogs" and "evil workers") who attempted to pervert the gospel by sanctifying the cutting of the flesh—an external sign of the old covenant—over the circumcision of the heart that rejoiced in Christ Jesus as Savior—a sign of the new covenant. With these words, he was speaking of a religious system out of touch, out of tune and focused on the wrong things. Mutilating your body doesn't make you God's child.

False Circumcision involves putting confidence in the flesh. For example:

» Rituals and traditions

» Physical mutilation (3:2)

» Image, status and personal qualifications (3:4-6)

» Self-effort (3:9)

Our flesh can be useful to the Lord, yet we are to put no confidence in the flesh. While **False Circumcision** puts confidence in the flesh, **True Circumcision** involves putting confidence in Christ. For example:

» Having faith in Christ alone for salvation and true righteousness (3:8-9)

» Seeing life's success in proper perspective to knowing Christ (3:8)

» Recognizing that Christ is of surpassing value to anything else (3:3, 8)

» Is a matter of a changed heart, not external legalistic rituals (3:3)

» Includes only those who worship in the Spirit of God (3:3)

"Religious people don't have to worship. They just have to be loyal. On the other hand, those who are in relationship and have an ongoing relationship of His presence, are compelled to worship. There's a difference between pageantry and worship in the Spirit."[82]

It is not related to where or when you worship, but how—in Spirit and in truth. Worship should be the delight of the church. In worship, we attribute to God His immeasurable worth, and we recognize the beauty of His grace and presence.

The Holy Spirit is able to expand our minds and hearts to accommodate and express true worship. Through the power of the Holy Spirit there is ongoing metamorphosis going on in our lives. He will take us further and higher than we have ever been before, if we allow Him.

Paul is proclaiming that there is nothing you can do through the flesh to earn His salvation.

Look up the following passages: Matthew 26:41; John 6:63; Romans 8:7; 1 Corinthians 1:26 and Galatians 5:19. What do they have to say about putting confidence in the flesh for salvation?

_____

_____

_____

_____

_____

Think about some ways you have put confidence in the flesh. How safe have you found that to be?

Why is there no safety when one puts confidence in the flesh?

_____

_____

_____

Look up the following passages: Romans 3:23; Romans 6:23-24; Romans 8:3, 5, 13; 2 Corinthians 10:3 and Galatians 6:8. What do they have to say about placing confidence in Christ alone and relying on the Spirit?

_____

_____

_____

_____

_____

Why is there rejoicing when one places confidence in Christ alone for salvation?

_____

_____

_____

_____

MEDITATE

Re-read this devotion and meditate on its implications for your life.

What is the Lord telling you?

_____

_____

_____

_____

_____

_____

_____

MEMORIZE

Review the personalized versions of Philippians 1:2, 6, 9, 18, 21, 27, 2:4-5, 11, 14 and 16 below, and repeat them every day.

Grace and peace are mine from God my Father and the Lord Jesus Christ.

He who began a good work in me will perfect it until the day of Christ Jesus.

I will walk in love and righteousness based on real knowledge and discernment of His glory.

As Christ is proclaimed, I will rejoice. For me, to live is Christ, to die is gain!

I will stand firm in one spirit, with one mind, working to further the gospel, thinking of others as more important than myself, having Christ's servant attitude.

That every tongue should confess that Jesus Christ is Lord, to the glory of God the Father.

I will do all without grumbling or disputing, holding fast and holding forth the Word of life.

DAY 2
REJOICING'S RIGHTEOUSNESS
Philippians 3:4-10

4 *although I myself might have confidence even in the flesh.*

If anyone else has a mind to put confidence in the flesh, I far more:

    5 *circumcised the eighth day,*

      of the nation of Israel,

        of the tribe of Benjamin,

          a Hebrew of Hebrews;

            as to the Law, a Pharisee;

        6 *as to zeal, a persecutor of the church;*

      as to the righteousness which is in the Law, found blameless.

    7 *But whatever things were gain to me,*

      those things I have counted as loss for the sake of Christ.

        8 *More than that,*

      I count all things to be loss

in view of the **surpassing value** *of knowing Christ Jesus my Lord,*

for whom **I have suffered the loss of all things,**

  and count them but **rubbish**

    in order that I may gain Christ,

      9 *and may be found in Him,*

        not having a righteousness of my own derived from the Law,

          but that which is through faith in Christ,

        the **righteousness** *which comes from God*

      on the **basis of faith,**

10 *that I may* **know** *Him,*

  And the **power of His resurrection**

    and the **fellowship of His sufferings,**

      being **conformed** *to His death;*

Paul had impeccable pedigree and upbringing, under Jewish standards. He had been born into the right family, followed the right traditions, been educated in the right schools, hung out with the right society and had acted in ways that society admired when he persecuted the church, which they thought taught heresy. If there were two words to describe the list that Paul provides in verses 4-6, it would be "status symbols." These qualifications would be impressive to the Jews, especially Jewish leaders. In their minds,

God Himself would also be impressed. Surely, a man with this résumé could stand confidently before God on the basis of his own merit! "Not so," said Paul, *"in view of the surpassing value of knowing Christ Jesus my Lord, for whom I have suffered the loss of all things, and count them but rubbish in order that I may gain Christ."* The salvation of God is based on grace, not race.

Paul counted those "status symbols" as *"rubbish"* in view of what?

_____

_____

What does *"surpassing value"* mean?

_____

_____

_____

Certainly, image and "status symbols" are not viewed as rubbish (dung) by the world. These are things individuals may even give their lives for. They may become so stressed by overworking to get the things of this world that they sacrifice their health. "Status symbols" are things that people may give their lives for because they do not have the right perspective. Their lives have gotten out of balance. They have not given time to that which is of *"surpassing value":* knowing Christ Jesus as Lord.

The fleeting nature of success is well-illustrated in societal examples. Today's respected celebrity may become tomorrow's drug addict, bankrupt professional, divorcée, box office catastrophe, media spectacle, talk show fodder or prison cellmate. In the sport's arena, even a celebrated professional athlete is just one fumble away from public humiliation. Without a doubt, the greatest indication of the fleeting nature of personal status and success is death.

This is not to say that there is no place for status. Status can open doors of opportunity. Certainly our status is raised in other people's eyes when we lead successful endeavors. Our status is raised when we show ourselves to be people of our word, wise in our dealings. As we demonstrate godly character, we gain status before our brothers and sisters in Christ. We may even have an ability or experience that propels us to public notoriety. Perhaps our God-inspired business savvy enables us to build a large respected company. Maybe an act of heroism pushes us to the forefront. It could be that we write a bestseller or win an award. It could just be that we are put into a respected leadership role in our church or community. Whatever it is, Paul's words urge us to keep it all in perspective. Status is fleeting. The rewards of knowing Christ are not.

What had Paul lost for the surpassing value of knowing Christ (3:4-6)?

_____

What had Paul gained (3:8-12)?

_____

_____

Had Paul gained more than he had lost? Why?

_____

_____

Does a person's positive impact suffer when an improper perspective leads to an inflated ego and prideful behavior? How does this negatively impact business associates, friends and family?

_____

_____

_____

In view of the above, what positive benefits can follow a proper perspective as one trusts Christ alone for salvation and allows Him to take charge of every area of one's life (4:8)?

_____

_____

_____

There's so much to know of Him. *"The power of His resurrection"* is another way of communicating, "there's nothing beyond His redemptive purposes." Paul was saying, "I want to know You and the power of Your resurrection. You can change Rome, and if I know You and walk in Your power, I can change Rome, too." *(It's interesting to note that Rome fell to the church while Constantine was in power.)* If you know Christ and the power of His resurrection, there is nothing too difficult for you.

Paul had fallen head over heels in love with Jesus. "Jesus filled his focus."[83]

"If you can take Him or leave Him, you are dating Him. But God does not want us to have a casual love for Him. He wants that love to so grab hold of our life that we don't want to let go."[84] So, we need to ask ourselves, "Are we in love, or are we in a continual state of dating Him? We must be in love with Him to walk our destiny potential, fully. We must live and walk in resurrection power to make the greatest impact.

MEDITATE

Re-read this devotion and meditate on its implications for your life.

What is the Lord telling you?

_____

_____

_____

_____

_____

_____

_____

MEMORIZE

Memorize the personalized versions of Philippians 1:2, 6, 9, 18, 21, 27, 2:4-5, 11, 14, 16 and 3:8 below, and repeat them every day.

Grace and peace are mine from God my Father and the Lord Jesus Christ.

He who began a good work in me will perfect it until the day of Christ Jesus.

I will walk in love and righteousness based on real knowledge and discernment of His glory.

As Christ is proclaimed, I will rejoice. For me, to live is Christ, to die is gain!

I will stand firm in one spirit, with one mind, working to further the gospel, thinking of others as more important than myself, having Christ's servant attitude.

That every tongue should confess that Jesus Christ is Lord, to the glory of God the Father.

I will do all without grumbling or disputing, holding fast and holding forth the Word of life.

I will rejoice in the surpassing value of knowing Christ Jesus our Lord.

DAY 3
REJOICING'S FOCUS
Philippians 3:11-16

11 *in order that I may attain to the resurrection from the dead.*

    12 *Not that I have already obtained it, or have already become perfect,*

        *but **I press on***

            in order that I may lay hold of that for which also I was laid hold of by Christ Jesus.

    13 *Brethren, I do not regard myself as having laid hold of it yet;*

        but one thing I do:

            forgetting what lies behind

      *and **reaching forward** to what lies ahead,*

  14 ***I press on** toward the goal for the **prize** of the **upward call** of God in Christ Jesus.*

15 *Let us therefore, as many as are **perfect**, have **this attitude**;*

    *and if in anything you have a **different** attitude,*

      God will reveal that also to you;

  16 *however, let us keep living by that **same standard to which we have attained**.*

In verses 10-14, Paul relates his spiritual journey to a race of eternal significance. This was something the Philippians could well appreciate, since they were very familiar with the laws and events connected with the contests of the famous Olympian games.

THE ANCIENT OLYMPIAN GAMES

The ancient Olympian Games were a series of athletic competitions held for spectators who represented various city-states of Ancient Greece. Earliest records indicate that they began in 776 BC in Olympia, Greece, and were celebrated until 393 AD. The winner's prizes were olive wreaths, palm branches and wool ribbons. However, the winners turned into celebrities and often had benefits like free food for the rest of their life and were privileged by being allowed first entry into the theaters. Back home, some winners received material prizes worth money.[85]

"Athlete" is a Greek word meaning, "one who competes for a prize" and is related to two other words, *athlos* meaning contest and *athlon* meaning prize.[86]

Before they were allowed to compete, athletes were required to complete intense training for ten months prior to the games. Epictetus, an ancient Stoic philosopher describes it this way in his "Golden Sayings:"

> "You would fain be victor at the Olympic games, you say. Yes, but weigh the conditions, weigh the consequences; then and then only, lay to your hand—if it be for your profit. You must live by rule, submit to diet, abstain from dainty meats, exercise your body perforce at stated hours, in heat or in cold; drink no cold water, nor, it may be, wine. In a word, you must surrender yourself wholly to your trainer, as though to a physician."[87]

Before competing, the athletes took an oath, as did the judges. They promised to compete in an honorable way, abiding by the rules. Cheating seems to have been rare at the ancient Olympics, which were held every four years. It is assumed there were some cheaters, but the judges were considered honest, and in general, so were the athletes. Cheating was partly deterred by the possibility of flogging and stiff fines.[88]

Running was the only sport competition during the first 13 Olympics. The race length was about 85 meters. Later, longer races (365 meters and 2 km) were included. In 708 BC, pentathlon and wrestling were included; in 688 BC, boxing; and in 680 BC, chariot racing. When the Romans gained domination over the Greeks, the Games gradually lost their importance. During Emperor Nero's reign, slaves competed for their lives fighting against wild animals in the place of free citizens.[89]

THE CHRISTIAN'S RACE

The *"prize"* that Paul spoke of was the *"upward call"* of God in Jesus Christ (3:14). This prize would be the glorious resurrection of the saints (3:11). It was at that point that saints would see the completion of their spiritual and physical perfection (3:12). Until that time, Christians could be perfect (3:15) in the sense that they were trusting in Christ alone for their salvation, were applying themselves to know Him and to be like Him, and as they were daily studying His Word and learning to rely on the guidance and control of the Holy Spirit.

Twice in these verses, Paul talks about *"pressing on"* (3:12, 14) toward the prize. Meditate on verses 10-16. In view of those verses, write out what "pressing on" seems to mean.

_____

_____

_____

_____

_____

"Pressing on" takes effort. There is a sense of "Do not give up! Keep going, even though trouble may come! Press on to know Him and to experience all that salvation has brought by His blood. Press through the difficulties. Do not let them stop you from completing the course and getting the prize!"

PHILIPPIANS 4:13-14
Brethren, I do not regard myself as having laid hold of it yet; but one thing I do: forgetting what lies behind and reaching forward to what lies ahead, I press on toward the goal for the prize of the upward call of God in Christ Jesus.

Pressing on involves forgetting what lies behind. In other words, do not live in the past. Let the past go and press forward to what He has for you in the future. He has great things for you. Where you are in this life is not where you will be. He is not finished with you yet. What we have here on the earth is not all there is. As Christians, we have hope of a better tomorrow and of eternal life. Live in hope, not in regret.

What is it that you need to let go of from the past? What do you need to focus on? What can you rejoice in? (You may want to go ahead and read Philippians 4 at this point.)

_____

_____

_____

_____

_____

_____

"Pressing on" involves moving forward in your Christian experience. It means not allowing that love for Him to grow cold. It involves spending time in His Presence, continuously, instead of living on past experiences. There needs to be an ongoing sense of His Presence. In the Old Testament, Israel would have been happy to camp by any old oasis, because it was good to look at. They were continuously tempted to return to Egypt, because it was familiar. God had much better things in store for them. He wanted to take them to the Promised Land!

Paul did not want to just imagine, from afar, what it might be to know Him. He wanted to know Him close up and dynamically. True love is based on knowledge, not imagination. Know Him continuously so that, every day, you can enter into the Promised Land of His Presence. You cannot know a person by just one encounter, dynamic though it might be. Ongoing relationship is an ongoing process.

MEDITATE

Re-read this devotion and meditate on its implications for your life.

What is the Lord telling you?

_____

_____

_____

_____

_____

_____

_____

MEMORIZE

Memorize the personalized versions of Philippians 1:2, 6, 9, 18, 21, 27, 2:4-5, 11, 14, 16, 3:8 and 14 below, and repeat them every day.

Grace and peace are mine from God my Father and the Lord Jesus Christ.

He who began a good work in me will perfect it until the day of Christ Jesus.

I will walk in love and righteousness based on real knowledge and discernment of His glory.

As Christ is proclaimed, I will rejoice. For me, to live is Christ, to die is gain!

I will stand firm in one spirit, with one mind, working to further the gospel, thinking of others as more important than myself, having Christ's servant attitude.

That every tongue should confess that Jesus Christ is Lord, to the glory of God the Father.

I will do all without grumbling or disputing, holding fast and holding forth the Word of life.

I will rejoice in the surpassing value of knowing Christ Jesus our Lord.

I will press on toward the goal for the prize of the upward call of God in Christ Jesus.

Day 4
Rejoicing's Pattern
Philippians 3:15-19

15 *Let us therefore, as many as are **perfect**,*

>*have **this attitude**;*

>>*and if in anything you have a **different** attitude,*

>>>*God will reveal that also to you;*

>>**16** *however, let us keep living by that **same standard to which we have attained**.*

>**17** *Brethren, join in following **my example**,*

>>*and observe those who walk according to the **pattern** you have in us.*

>>>**18** *For many walk, of whom I often told you,*

>>*and now tell you even weeping,*

>*that they are **enemies of the cross** of Christ,*

19 *whose **end is destruction**,*

>*whose **god is their appetite**,*

>>*and whose **glory is in their shame**,*

>>>*who **set their minds on earthly things**.*

So what does Paul mean when he follows, *"I press on toward the goal for the prize of the upward call ..."* with *"Let us therefore, as many as are perfect have this attitude ..."*? In this verse, *"perfect"* does not mean without flaw. It means: be mature in understanding, think as adults not children, thoroughly instructed in the things of God, not captured by false teaching, intensely focused on eternal life, not halting until the race is done (see also 1 Corinthians 14:20; 1 Corinthians 2:6; Hebrews 5:14).[90]

To grow in knowledge has to do with growing in responsibility. It's not what we are that impresses God, but what we can be!

"Perfect"

(téleios). From "telos"; complete (in various applications of labor, growth, mental and moral character, etc.); neuter as noun, with "ho" completeness (of full age, man or perfect.)[91]

Paul continues by saying, *"and if in anything you have a different attitude, God will reveal that also to you"* (3:16). If you have not yet fully embraced the gospel message and spirit, God will reveal truth to you—if you are open to receive it.

It is at this point that Paul urges his beloved followers to continue to move forward in their Christian lives: *"let us keep living by that same standard to which we have attained."* He did not want them to lose ground, but to keep the finish line in view, minding the same thing, always focused on the glorious prize ahead—eternal life and complete transformation. He tells them to follow his example and teaching.

What kind of example had Paul set before the believers at Philippi? Where had he come from? Had he ever been an enemy of the cross? List some of the characteristics of his teaching and life.

_____

_____

_____

_____

What has impressed you most about Paul's life?

_____

_____

_____

The Christian life is meant to be lived as a great adventure as we continue to grow and face new challenges and opportunities to live our destiny. It's not to be a stagnant life.

In verses 18-19, Paul wept as he talked about negative examples: *"enemies of the cross of Christ."* Those enemies were Jews who taught that it was necessary to incorporate circumcision and other ordinances of the law, as a requirement with the gospel, before anyone could be justified before God. They were enemies of the complete nature of Jesus' ultimate sacrifice, which was more than enough. Without the cross there is no conversion.

A church without the cross is not a Christian church. The purpose of these *"enemies"* was to destroy the truth and dilute the power of the resurrection. Paul was warning Christians, "Be careful who you follow."

What else does Paul tell us about these false teachers in verses 18 and 19?

_____

_____

_____

_____

Paul was deeply grieved over these men because they had diverted many from God's plan of salvation, and because they would, themselves, be lost because of their personal deception. These men and their followers would never experience **Surrender's Joy** or be able to live their destiny. Instead, they lived only to eat, drink and be merry. They gained money and notoriety by preaching a doctrine which flattered the passions of their hearers, much to their shame *("Their glory is in their shame")*. They had an earthly mind that focused on the ungodly things of this world.

Are there any ways that you are like these men over whom Paul wept? How?

_____

_____

_____

It's time to take out the garbage.

Now, re-read 3:8-16. How focused are you on the prize? What do you need to do to keep yourself focused and growing? What do you think God wants for your life? What do you want?

_____

_____

_____

_____

_____

What is God saying to you? Write a prayer below.

_____

_____

_____

_____

> *The Christian life is meant to be lived as a great adventure, as we continue to grow and face new challenges and opportunities to live our destiny. It's not to be a stagnant life.*

MEDITATE

Re-read this devotion and meditate on its implications for your life.

What is the Lord telling you?

_____

_____

_____

_____

_____

_____

_____

MEMORIZE

Review the personalized versions of Philippians 1:2, 6, 9, 18, 21, 27, 2:4-5, 11, 14, 16, 3:8 and 14 below, and repeat them every day.

Grace and peace are mine from God my Father and the Lord Jesus Christ.

He who began a good work in me will perfect it until the day of Christ Jesus.

I will walk in love and righteousness based on real knowledge and discernment of His glory.

As Christ is proclaimed, I will rejoice. For me, to live is Christ, to die is gain!

I will stand firm in one spirit, with one mind, working to further the gospel, thinking of others as more important than myself, having Christ's servant attitude.

That every tongue should confess that Jesus Christ is Lord, to the glory of God the Father.

I will do all without grumbling or disputing, holding fast and holding forth the Word of life.

I will rejoice in the surpassing value of knowing Christ Jesus our Lord.

I will press on toward the goal for the prize of the upward call of God in Christ Jesus.

DAY 5
REJOICING'S CITIZENSHIP
Philippians 3:20-21

20 *For our **citizenship** is in heaven,*
   from which also we eagerly wait for a Savior,
      the Lord Jesus Christ;
   21 *who will **transform** the body of our humble state*
*into **conformity** with the body of **His glory**,*
   *by the **exertion of the power***
      *that He has even to **subject all things to Himself**.*

As he writes this letter, the Apostle Paul seems to stand on the edge of eternity with the past, present and future world in view. He has spoken about the place where the Christian starts the race (1:6-7). Out of a deep emotional concern that they successfully finish the race, he has spent most of the time writing about the course on which the Christian is to run. He wants his beloved friends to obtain the prize.

Separated from his friends, chained between two guards, Paul is emotional as he attempts to guide the Philippi believers from afar. He knows they are trying to maneuver hindrances, dangers and temptations on the path and encourages them to stand united so they can benefit from each other's strengths. In discussing the path of their race, he urges them to keep focused on the prize ("Well done, thou good and faithful servant") and the future transformation of their bodies.

The word *"citizenship"* signifies the administration, government or form of a republic or state; or the inhabitants of any city or place; or a society of persons living in the same place and under the same rules and laws.[92]

Those false Jewish teachers only had an earthly city and societal rights with others who focused on earthly things and whose appetites were their god. In comparison, we have a heavenly city, with rights and privileges which are heavenly and eternal! On the other hand, our society or fellowship is with God the Father, Son and Spirit, and the true church, His Body. We have His Spirit who enables us to be and live beyond our natural limitations to walk our destiny and live in **Surrender's Joy**. We need to remember where our true citizenship lies! This world is only a temporary dwelling place. **This is cause for rejoicing!**

We can also rejoice in the fact that God will transform our earthly limited body into a glorious one by the same dynamic power with which He created us in the first place (3:21) and by which He subjects all things to Himself!

Like it or not, our current body will die. Thankfully, though, our new body will have the likeness, immortality and glory of the glorified humanity of Jesus Christ, therefore unleashing amazing eternal heavenly possibilities to be enjoyed at the right hand of God.

This glorious transformation was a subject of the highest joy and confidence among the early Christians, as it should be for us. This earth was not their home; nor is it ours. Its difficulties are only temporary. We are running for a prize of an upward call of Christ Jesus, even as they were!

As the apostle looks at the present and future worlds, he sees the earthly one as preparation for the heavenly one yet to be attained. One world is seen as the starting place, where the Christian begins his race, while the other is the goal at which his course ends and where he receives the prize. One is the course over which the Christian is to run. He is not alone as he runs this course which includes temptations, difficulties and dangers. Jesus runs with him and is also at the end, calling him to the finish line.

> *"As Christians, we are people of two dimensions.*
> *We are people of now and eternity."* [93]

The nearer a genuine Christian comes to the edge of eternity, the more they see the dawning light and glory of the eternal world as the concerns of the world fade away.

List some of the difficulties you have faced up to this point.

_____

_____

_____

_____

_____

_____

_____

Read 3:1, 8, 9-16, 20-21 and 4:1. How would things have been different if you had kept the proper perspective during those difficulties?

_____

_____

_____

_____

_____

Learn to sing even when everything is not beautiful. Even though there may be rain outside, there can still be sunshine in your heart. We want to know Him, not so we can brag about it, but so we can reveal Him to those around us. Learn to walk in Christ, empowered by His Spirit, so you can reveal Him ... even when it's raining outside.

MEDITATE

Meditate on today's devotional. Write a declaration based on these verses and post it someplace where you will see it regularly.

_____

_____

_____

_____

_____

_____

_____

MEMORIZE

Review the personalized versions of Philippians 1:2, 6, 9, 18, 21, 27, 2:4-5, 11, 14, 16, 3:8 and 14 below, and repeat them every day.

Grace and peace are mine from God my Father and the Lord Jesus Christ.

He who began a good work in me will perfect it until the day of Christ Jesus.

I will walk in love and righteousness based on real knowledge and discernment of His glory.

As Christ is proclaimed, I will rejoice. For me, to live is Christ, to die is gain!

I will stand firm in one spirit, with one mind, working to further the gospel, thinking of others as more important than myself, having Christ's servant attitude.

That every tongue should confess that Jesus Christ is Lord, to the glory of God the Father.

I will do all without grumbling or disputing, holding fast and holding forth the Word of life.

I will rejoice in the surpassing value of knowing Christ Jesus our Lord.

I will press on toward the goal for the prize of the upward call of God in Christ Jesus.

THE EPISTLE OF PAUL THE APOSTLE

PHILIPPIANS.

CHAPTER I.

WEEK FIVE
SURRENDER'S PEACE

Philippians 4:1-23

Day 1 – Peace's Foundation (4:1)   113

Day 2 – Peace with Others (4:2-3)   118

Day 3 – Peace Principles (4:4-7)   122

Day 4 – Peace Principles *(continued)* (4:4-9)   127

Day 5 – Peace with Circumstances (4:10-23)   134

UPWARD LIVING IN A WORLD GONE MAD

SURRENDER'S JOY

A Study of Philippians

Week Five

Surrender's Peace

1 *Therefore, my beloved brethren*
    (whom I long to see, my joy and crown,)
        *So **stand firm in the Lord**, my beloved.*

            2 *I urge Euodia and I urge Syntyche to*
                ***live in harmony in the Lord**.*

                3 *Indeed, true comrade, I ask you also to*
                    ***help** these women who have **shared my struggle in the cause of the gospel**,*
                together with Clement also,
            *and the rest of my **fellow workers**, whose names are in the book of life.*

4 ***Rejoice in the Lord always**; again I will say, rejoice!*

    5 ***Let your forbearing spirit be known to all men. The Lord is near**.*

        6 ***Be anxious for nothing**,*
            *but **in everything by prayer and supplication with thanksgiving***
        ***let your requests be made known to God**.*

7 *And the **peace of God**,*
    *(which **surpasses all comprehension**,)*
        *shall **guard your hearts and your minds** in Christ Jesus.*

8 *Finally, brethren,*
    *whatever is **true**,*
        *whatever is **honorable**,*
            *whatever is **right**,*
                *whatever is **pure**,*
                    *whatever is **lovely**,*
                        *whatever is of **good repute**,*
                *if there is any **excellence***
            *and if anything **worthy of praise**,*
        *let your mind **dwell** on these things.*

9 *The things you have **learned** and **received** and **heard** and **seen** in me,*
        ***practice these** things; and the God of peace shall be with you.*

10 *But I* **rejoiced** *in the Lord greatly,*

  that now at last you have revived your concern for me;

 indeed, you were concerned before, but you lacked opportunity.

11 *Not that I speak from want;*

  for I have learned to be **content** *in whatever* **circumstances** *I am.*

   12 *I know how to get along with* **humble means,**

    and I also know how to live in **prosperity;**

     in any and every circumstance

      I have learned the **secret of being filled** *and* **going hungry,**

    both of having **abundance** *and* **suffering need.**

  13 *I can do all things through Him who strengthens me.*

14 *Nevertheless,*

  you have done well to share with me in my affliction.

   15 *And you yourselves also know, Philippians,*

    that at the first preaching of the gospel, after I departed from Macedonia,

     no church shared with me in the matter of **giving** *and* **receiving** *but you alone;*

   16 *for even in Thessalonica you sent a gift more than once for my needs.*

   17 *Not that I seek the gift itself, but I seek for the profit which increases to your account.*

    18 *But I have received everything in full,*

     and have an **abundance;** *I am* **amply supplied,**

     having received from Epaphroditus **what you have sent,**

  a fragrant aroma, an acceptable sacrifice, well-pleasing to God.

19 **And my God shall supply all your needs according to His riches in glory in Christ Jesus.**

   20 **Now to our God and Father be the glory forever and ever. Amen.**

   21 *Greet every saint in Christ Jesus. The brethren who are with me greet you.*

  22 *All the saints greet you, especially those of Caesar's household.*

23 *The* **grace** *of the Lord Jesus Christ be with your spirit.*

DAY 1
PEACE'S FOUNDATION
Philippians 4:1

1 *Therefore, my beloved brethren*
 (whom I long to see, my joy and crown,)
  So **stand firm in the Lord***, my beloved.*

Paul dearly loved these Philippians. He is very expressive of that deep regard in this short verse. Twice he calls them *"beloved,"* or more correctly *"dearly beloved."* "The expression is one word in the Greek—the word which is used for God's divine and self-sacrificial love. It is plural in number. Paul loves all of these saints individually and with a love produced in his heart by the Holy Spirit."[94]

The apostle calls them his *"joy and crown."* He rejoiced that these dear ones, who had been converted under him, had continued to grow in their faith and had participated with him in sharing the gospel message with others. They were some of the fruit of his life's work. He would be able to present them, as a crown, to Christ at his own graduation day, because they had continued in the faith. They were indication that he had lived a fruitful life.

The particular Greek word for *"crown"* here refers to the victor's garland or wreath placed upon the head of the victor in the athletic games. It was given for military valor. It was used at festal occasions as an expression of gladness. This garland was woven of oak leaves, ivy, myrtle, olive, or of flowers, violets or roses. Paul's garland of victory in his Christian service was composed of the Philippian saints whom he had won to the Lord Jesus.[95]

Paul longed to hear from these spiritual children and to see them. Even more, he longed to know that they were well—physically and in spirit. Locked in prison, chained between two guards, he had much time for meditation. Very likely, he would tenderly smile as their faces came to mind. To hear of their spiritual health would bring him great joy. The numerous terms of endearment in this verse show his tender regard for them and are an expression of his earnest concern for their welfare. He was deeply concerned about their increasing danger, because they lived under the Roman rule of the evil and increasingly unstable Nero.

The use of the word *"therefore"* shows the strong connection of this verse to the ending verses of chapter three. In view of the fact that the Philippians were actually citizens of heaven and had the hope of a coming Savior, they were to stand fast in the Lord. They had His armor and God Himself for their support.

Translation: *Therefore, my brothers, individually loved ones, and individually and passionately longed for, my joy and my victor's festal garland, thus be standing firm in the Lord, beloved ones.*[96]

This is the second time Paul has told them to *"stand firm."* The first time was in Philippians 1:27. That time, though, the emphasis was on unity. They were to *"stand firm, united ...."* Here, the emphasis is on the foundation on which they were to stand, Jesus Christ. They were to stand fast in the Lord's service and in His strength (see Ephesians 5:13-14).

As we stated earlier, this could be related to the concept of soldiers standing firm in battle or of believers condemned and fighting for their lives in a Roman amphitheater (Ephesians 6:13; 1 Corinthians 4:9). *"To stand firm"* could also be expressed negatively as "not to be moved," "not to change" or "not to give up."

Take some time to meditate on definitions for *"stand"* and *"firm,"* as given below, in some of the online English dictionaries.

STAND

- To assume or maintain an upright position as specified: *stand straight; stand to one side.*
- To maintain an upright or vertical position on a base or support: *The urn stands on a pedestal.*
- To remain stable, upright or intact: *The old school still stands.*
- To remain valid, effective or unaltered: *The agreement stands.*
- To take up or maintain a specified position, altitude or course: *He stands on his earlier offer. We will stand firm.*[97]

FIRM

- Marked by firm determination or resolution; not shakable; "firm convictions"; "a firm mouth"; "steadfast resolve"; "a man of unbendable ..."
- Not soft or yielding to pressure; "a firm mattress"; "solid ground": *The snow was firm underfoot.*
- Strong and sure; "a firm grasp"; "gave a strong pull on the rope."
- Not subject to revision or change; "a firm contract"; "a firm offer."
- (Relating to a person's physical features) not shaking or trembling; "a firm step": *His voice was firm and confident.*
- Not liable to fluctuate or especially to fall: *Stocks are still firm.*
- Securely established; "holds a firm position as the country's leading poet."
- Tauten: become taut or tauter: *Your muscles will firm when you exercise regularly. The rope tautened.*
- Fast; securely fixed in place: *The post was still firm after being hit by the car.*
- With resolute determination: *We firmly believed it. You must stand firm.*[98]

FIRM (fûrm)

adj. **firm·er, firm·est**

- Resistant to externally applied pressure.

- Marked by or indicating the tone and resiliency of healthy tissue: *firm muscles.*

- Securely fixed in place: *Despite being hit by the car, the post was still firm.*

- Indicating or possessed of determination or resolution: *a firm voice.*

- Constant; steadfast: *a firm ally.*

- Not subject to change; fixed and definite: *a firm bargain; a firm offer.*

- Unfluctuating; steady: *Stock prices are still firm.*

- Strong and sure: *a firm grasp.*

- Without wavering; resolutely: *stand firm.*[99]

Meditate on the above comments and information for a moment. What is the Lord saying to you relative to your life?

_____

_____

_____

Below are some other scriptures in which Paul tells the believers to "stand fast" or "stand firm."

1. **Acts 14:22**
   Paul was *"strengthening the souls of the disciples, encouraging them to continue in the faith."*

2. **1 Corinthians 15:58**
   Paul encouraged fellow believers by saying, *"Be steadfast, immovable, always abounding in the work of the Lord, knowing that your toil is not in vain in the Lord."*

3. **Galatians 5:1**
   To help the believers avoid falling back into Jewish legalism, Paul said, *"It was for freedom that Christ set us free; therefore keep standing firm and do not be subject again to a yoke of slavery."*

4. **Ephesians 6:11**
   "Put on the full armor of God, that you may be able to stand firm against the schemes of the devil."

5. **1 Thessalonians 3:8**
   "For now we really live, if you stand firm in the Lord." Paul's heart leapt with joy when he saw stability in other believers, and so should our hearts leap over the same thing.

6. **2 Thessalonians 2:15**

   "Stand firm and hold to the traditions which you were taught, whether by word of mouth or by letter from us." The believers were to hold fast to the biblical truths they learned from Paul.

The other apostles also taught about standing firm. For example, Peter said, *"Be on your guard lest, being carried away by the error of unprincipled men, you fall from your own steadfastness"* (2 Peter 3:17).

To stand firm in the Lord means:

1. To stand upright rather than in a position of acquittal (Romans 14:4).

2. To stand in the faith, by adherence to it (1 Corinthians 16:13).

3. To stand in freedom from legal bondage (Galatians 5:1).

4. To stand in one spirit (Philippians 1:27).

5. To stand in the Apostle's teaching (2 Thessalonians 2:15).

6. To not compromise your Christian testimony by allowing yourselves to be overwhelmed by trials or temptation (Ephesians 5:11).

7. To be even and steady in your walk with Him, and close and constant unto the end (Philippians 4:1; 1 Thessalonians 3:8).

8. To stand fast in His strength and by His grace; not trusting in yourselves or your own sufficiency (Philippians 4:1; 1 Thessalonians 3:8).

9. To be strong in the Lord, and in the power of His might (Philippians 4:1; 1 Thessalonians 3:8).

Review the material in this devotional. What changes need to take place in your thoughts, attitudes and actions? How do you foresee that this will change your life?

_____

_____

_____

_____

_____

_____

_____

MEMORIZE

Review the personalized versions of Philippians 1:2, 6, 9, 18, 21, 27, 2:4-5, 11, 14, 16, 3:8 and 14 below, and repeat them every day.

Grace and peace are mine from God my Father and the Lord Jesus Christ.

He who began a good work in me will perfect it until the day of Christ Jesus.

I will walk in love and righteousness based on real knowledge and discernment of His glory.

As Christ is proclaimed, I will rejoice. For me, to live is Christ, to die is gain!

I will stand firm in one spirit, with one mind, working to further the gospel, thinking of others as more important than myself, having Christ's servant attitude.

That every tongue should confess that Jesus Christ is Lord, to the glory of God the Father.

I will do all without grumbling or disputing, holding fast and holding forth the Word of life.

I will rejoice in the surpassing value of knowing Christ Jesus our Lord.

I will press on toward the goal for the prize of the upward call of God in Christ Jesus.

DAY 2
PEACE WITH OTHERS
Philippians 4:2-3

2 *I urge Euodia and I urge Syntyche to*
> *live in harmony in the Lord.*
>> **3** *Indeed, true comrade, I ask you also to*
>>> *help these women who have shared my struggle in the cause of the gospel,*
>> *together with Clement also,*
> *and the rest of my fellow workers, whose names are in the book of life.*

Have you ever found it hard to *"live in"* harmony? I admit it. I find it hard sometimes. Yet, this is just what we are asked to do.

It had been 12 years since Paul had founded the church at Philippi. Euodia and Syntyche, among the first converts, along with Lydia, had shared Paul's *"struggle in the cause of the gospel."* That their labor had been significant seems likely, for the church was founded during a critical time of danger and suffering. That he mentions them by name is important, for this is something he generally does only in greetings and the occasional mention of his coworkers. "One of the marks of enmity in polemical letters is that enemies are left unnamed, thus denigrated by anonymity."[100]

These two women would have been esteemed highly in the church because of their founding role with Lydia. They were loyal believers, good Christians who had lost their focus. Their conflict, small though it may have been, threatened not only the unity of this close-knit community, but its impact on the outside culture. Argumentative Christians don't shine. They look like everyone else!

Throughout his letter to Philippi, Paul pleads for unity. It is filled with phrases such as *"stand firm in one spirit,"* and *"contending as **one** man"* (1:27). Paul urged the believers there to make his joy complete by being *"like-minded, having the **same love**,"* and being *"one in spirit and purpose"* (2:2). In these verses, Paul entreats these two leaders to *agree with each other* (*phronein* – "have the same mindset") *in the Lord*.[101]

Earlier in the letter, Paul urges the church body to be different from those who do not know Christ (2:14-16). Today, we are urged to do the same. As Christians, we are to follow Christ's example of humility and forgiveness. We aren't to harbor grudges, but are to work hard to resolve conflicts. As we walk in **Surrender's Peace,** we will shine like stars in the darkness.

What do you think of when you hear the word *"harmony?"* If you're like me, you will think of music. Let's contrast the difference between harmony and disharmony. When I think of disharmony, I visualize children who are just learning to play an instrument or trying to play together in a band. Now, if you are a proud parent, you just grin and bear it during those required events. Externally, your children see a smiling face, while inside you are screaming for deliverance! Disharmony, in music, is hard to withstand for long.

Now, harmony is another matter. The harmonious blending of chords skillfully played by well-tuned and carefully directed instruments, is beautiful … even mesmerizing. Harmonious sound can carry you upward, while disharmony keeps you focused on the disharmony, making it difficult to focus upward.

Let's look at how the American Heritage Dictionary defines harmony:

HARMONY

1. Agreement in feeling or opinion; accord: *live in harmony.*
2. A pleasing combination of elements in a whole: *color harmony; the order and harmony of the universe.*
3. *Music*
   a. The study of the structure, progression and relation of chords.
   b. Simultaneous combination of notes in a chord.
   c. The structure of a work or passage as considered from the point of view of its chordal characteristics and relationships.
   d. A combination of sounds considered pleasing to the ear.
4. A collation of parallel passages, especially from the Gospels, with a commentary demonstrating their consonance and explaining their discrepancies.[102]

An orchestra is made up of many instruments, each one quite different. Yet, when each well-tuned (mature/growing/focused/well-founded) instrument is carefully following the director (God) and is playing a carefully written musical piece (God's plan), the harmonious blending gives a powerfully positive testimony to those listening.

As they had lost their focus, Euodia and Syntyche had lost their harmony. That disharmony came because they were out of harmony with the Lord. Working for the Lord must be balanced with time spent at the feet of the Lord for there to be harmony.

In his letter, Paul asked a coworker (*"true comrade"*) who was in Philippi to help Euodia and Syntyche to resolve their differences and restore harmony in the church. He wanted to make sure that nothing would interfere with that precious body of people successfully running the race. He didn't want anything to weaken their readiness to walk victoriously in a hostile world.

Christians are to remember that the world is watching! We are to reflect Him. Conflicts will arise, but we must not put our testimony in jeopardy by fighting among ourselves. We must be an example by following Christ's example, not acting based on self-interest, but obedience (Philippians 2:6-11). When we empty ourselves of self-interest, harmony can be restored. Let's remember Paul's words in Colossians 3:13-14. Bear with each other. Forgive grievances. Forgive as the Lord forgave us. As members of one body, we are called to peace.

Are you walking in harmony with the Lord? If you're not, why not?

_____

_____

_____

What habits/patterns have you maintained during times that you are walking in harmony?

_____

_____

_____

_____

Are you harboring bitterness toward anyone? Does that bitterness have anything to do with self-interest? How is it related?

_____

_____

_____

_____

What do you need to do, right now, to begin to live in harmony with God and others?

_____

_____

_____

_____

MEDITATE

Journal your thoughts and write out a plan to move into harmony.

_____

_____

_____

_____

_____

_____

_____

MEMORIZE

Review the personalized versions of Philippians 1:2, 6, 9, 18, 21, 27, 2:4-5, 11, 14, 16, 3:8 and 14 below, and repeat them every day.

Grace and peace are mine from God my Father and the Lord Jesus Christ.

He who began a good work in me will perfect it until the day of Christ Jesus.

I will walk in love and righteousness based on real knowledge and discernment of His glory.

As Christ is proclaimed, I will rejoice. For me, to live is Christ, to die is gain!

I will stand firm in one spirit, with one mind, working to further the gospel, thinking of others as more important than myself, having Christ's servant attitude.

That every tongue should confess that Jesus Christ is Lord, to the glory of God the Father.

I will do all without grumbling or disputing, holding fast and holding forth the Word of life.

I will rejoice in the surpassing value of knowing Christ Jesus our Lord.

I will press on toward the goal for the prize of the upward call of God in Christ Jesus.

DAY 3
PEACE PRINCIPLES
Philippians 4:4-7

4 *Rejoice in the Lord always;* *again I will say, rejoice!*

    5 Let your forbearing spirit be known to all men. The Lord is near.

        6 Be anxious for nothing,

            but **in everything by prayer and supplication with thanksgiving**

        let your requests be made known to God.

7 *And the* **peace of God,** *(which* **surpasses all comprehension,)**

    shall **guard** *your hearts and your minds in Christ Jesus.*

In his letter that has transcended the time in which it was written, Paul has spoken words straight from the mind and heart of God! Now, as he writes his concluding remarks, Paul wants to make sure his dear friends of the present (the Philippians) and of the future (us) completely understand the power of **Upward Living's** total surrender. Obviously, Paul had a premonition of the intense persecution that was to come to the Philippians. He also knew that crises come to people no matter the nation or time period, whether privileged or impoverished. Paul's command is the same for everyone, *"**Rejoice in the Lord always;** <u>again</u> I will say, **rejoice!**"*

It is important to note that rejoice *(chairete)* is in the present active imperative, as it was in 3:1, and it is repeated for emphasis. In other words, we are being commanded to rejoice continuously … always … every day … all the time … no matter what happens!

REJOICING'S FOCUS: THE LORD

We are to rejoice *in the Lord.* Paul is saying, "I've experienced the trials of life and I know what I'm saying. I've considered everything that can possibly happen. Still, I say, rejoice!" Our joy is independent of all things on earth because it has as its source the continual Presence of Christ. "The Christian can never lose his joy, because he can never lose Christ."[103] We cannot control everything that happens to us, but He can mold the ashes of that experience into beauty.

> ROMANS 8:28
> *And we know that God causes all things to work together for good to those who love God, to those who are called according to His purpose.*

REJOICING'S VISIBLE CHARACTER: GENTLENESS

Paul encourages us to be joyful and to, *"**Let your** (our) **forbearing** (gentle) **spirit be known to all men.**"* What is in our heart is to be seen by *everyone*—especially those outside the church. "The Greek word for gentleness *(epieikes)* refers to a spirit that is reasonable, fair-minded and charitable. It describes someone willing to yield his or her own rights to show consideration and gentleness to others." (Barton) The same word is used in 2 Corinthians 10:1 in discussing the *"meekness and gentleness of Christ."* Jesus never sacrificed truth in order to be gentle, but He always had a gentle spirit that often disarmed those set against Him."[104] The words *"at hand"* are from a Greek word meaning literally *"near."* The nearness of the Lord's return (the Rapture is in Paul's mind) and His daily abiding Presence with His children, enforces gentleness and is a cure for worry."[105]

REJOICING'S ENERGY: CONTINUAL PRESENCE

"Be anxious for nothing." The knowledge that the Lord's coming is near is a reminder to us that we are "just passing through." The troubles we face here are just temporary. They are part of something much bigger and more enduring—God's eternal plan and the fulfillment of our eternal destiny, to take place when we see Him face to face! When Paul speaks of God's "nearness" he is not just speaking about His return. He is speaking about His abiding Presence with His children.

Joy is not the absence of something, but the Presence of Someone. It springs forth from a heart that is committed. The discipline comes in rejoicing always. His faithfulness is not dependent on our ability to perform. Our ability to perform depends on His faithfulness. *"The Lord is near. Be anxious for nothing."* If the Lord is near, you can be anxious for nothing. He is our strength and shield. He is near. Everything that is of interest to us is of interest to Him.

"Anxious" relates to being in a continual state of anxiety, distracted by the things around us. Paul is saying, "Do not be continuously distracted." It's one thing to take a quick look, but another to dwell on a negative situation allowing negative emotions to suck the joy right out of you! We can't pretend that difficult situations aren't going to arise that will grab our attention for a moment. Often, it takes a lot of strength to take our eyes off of a situation, but we *must*. The root word for *"anxious"* means to *"pull apart."* Paul does not want Christians to allow themselves to be *pulled apart* by situations that arise.

"Be anxious for nothing." Do not allow yourself to be derailed by the problems of life. Do not allow the things of this world to distract you. If they are allowed to distract you, they will deter you from what you have been called to be and do for the glory of the Lord. Remember this: *Your sense of well-being is not to be found in any person's ability to perform, but in His ability to perform!*

The world situation is steadily deteriorating, as was prophesied. On the other hand, the church will shine like a light as long as we are focused on Him, reflecting His glory! Paul is saying, "Don't allow the distractions of the world to pull you apart and pull you away from your Christ focus." Shine beloved believer ... shine!

Where has your focus been? Have you been shining?

_____

_____

In Philippi, they had allowed themselves to focus on the wrong thing, the internal strife in their church. Their horizontal focus had dulled their shine. *"**Be anxious for nothing**, but **in everything** by **prayer and**

supplication with thanksgiving *let your requests be made known to God.*" We are to take all the energy that is used in worrying and put it into prayer. We are to pray about *everything*, not just some things. No request is too small or difficult. Everything is important to God. We are to pray *always*—in good times and bad—giving petitions and thanksgivings to God.

"The word for *prayer* is a general term meaning worshipful conversation with God, while *petition* refers to a prayer with a sense of need. These two words often appear together in Paul's writings."[106] *Thanksgiving* focuses on the attitude of our heart as we approach God. *Prayer* combats worry by re-directing our focus from what we lack to what we have and Who we belong to! We should approach God, thankful for the opportunity, His tremendous blessings given and for the certainty that He will answer us. When we focus on God's amazing love for us and the testimony of His many answered prayers, we will have no room to worry about whether He will continue to answer. *"Requests"* refer to directly asking God's help regarding specific needs. Prayer combats worry by building trust."[107]

Paul admonished the Thessalonians to *"pray continually"* (1 Thessalonians 5:17). Communication with God through prayer allows us to know Him better and to know His will and guidance for our lives."[108] Someone once said, "We can be careful for nothing, if we are prayerful about everything." If we walk in His nearness and pray continuously, we will be at peace.

> *Prayer not only changes things, it changes people.*

1 PETER 5:6-7
Humble yourselves, therefore, under the mighty hand of God, that He may exalt you at the proper time, casting all your anxiety upon Him, because He cares for you.

"Cast all your anxiety upon Him" so that your life's atmosphere will be peace.

REJOICING'S GUARD: PEACE

"And the peace of God, (which surpasses all comprehension,) shall guard your hearts and your minds in Christ Jesus." Individually and collectively, the church has a bodyguard—the peace of God. God wants to rule and reign in you so that there will be no discord in the secret places of your life. His abiding peace is available to those who abide in Him.

Jesus told us, *"Abide in Me, and I in you. As the branch cannot bear fruit of itself, unless it abides in the vine, so neither can you, unless you abide in Me. I am the vine, you are the branches; he who abides in Me, and I in him, he bears much fruit; for apart from Me you can do nothing. If anyone does not abide in Me, he is thrown away as a branch, and dries up; and they gather them, and cast them into the fire, and they are burned. If you abide in Me, and My words abide in you, ask whatever you wish, and it shall be done for you. By this is My Father glorified, that you bear much fruit, and so prove to be My disciples"* (John 15:4-9).

This peace is different from the world's temporary and shaky peace. It is an inner peace that Jesus promised to all those who follow Him: *"Peace I leave with you; My peace I give you. I do not give to you as the world gives. Do not let your hearts be troubled and do not be afraid"* (John 14:27). "True peace is not found in positive thinking, in absence of conflict or in good feelings; it comes from knowing that God is in control. Believers are given peace *with* God when they believe (Romans 5:1), and they have the inner quiet of the peace *of* God as they daily walk with Him."[109]

God's peace *surpasses all comprehension.* We simply cannot understand such peace. It is not a natural reaction to pain, trauma, loss or crises. It is not a peace that can be self-generated, for it is a gift from God alone. His peace cannot be understood, but it can be experienced and accepted in light of His great love for us.

God's peace acts as soldiers (guards) surrounding believers' hearts and minds, securing them against outside forces that threaten to destroy. Romans 16:20 indicates to us that it is a powerful peace, *"And the God of peace will soon crush Satan under your feet."* God is more than "Abba Father." He is Almighty God! He's more than a big, fuzzy teddy bear. He's the Creator of all things, and in Him all things hold together. He is God who will give us peace. Everything about God is a paradox. Our human mind simply cannot understand God. No man has seen God. Moses just saw part of God's glory and it was overwhelming!

EXODUS 33:18-23
Then Moses said, "I pray Thee, show me Thy glory!" And He said, "I Myself will make all My goodness pass before you, and will proclaim the name of the Lord before you; and I will be gracious to whom I will be gracious, and will show compassion on whom I will show compassion." But He said, "You cannot see My face, for no man can see Me and live!" Then the Lord said, "Behold, there is a place by Me, and you shall stand there on the rock; and it will come about, while My glory is passing by, that I will put you in the cleft of the rock and cover you with My hand until I have passed by. Then I will take My hand away and you shall see My back, but My face shall not be seen."

EXODUS 34:31-35
Then Moses called to them, and Aaron and all the rulers in the congregation returned to him; and Moses spoke to them. And afterward all the sons of Israel came near, and he commanded them to do everything that the Lord had spoken to him on Mount Sinai. When Moses had finished speaking with them, he put a veil over his face. But whenever Moses went in before the Lord to speak with Him, he would take off the veil until he came out; and whenever he came out and spoke to the sons of Israel what he had been commanded, the sons of Israel would see the face of Moses, that the skin of Moses' face shone. So Moses would replace the veil over his face until he went in to speak with Him.

Our world has a limited understanding of the Bible, but they do not understand Him. It is the Spirit who reveals Him and illuminates His Word to those who want to know Him. In the church, it is easy to get caught up in being a part of the church without being a part of Him. Whenever we lose the reality of relationship, we can begin to find our solace only in the comfortable rituals and traditions of religion. *"Guard"* was a term the Philippians would well understand, for there were military guards all around their city. We can rest assured that, regardless of what else He is doing in our lives, He is guarding it.

MEDITATE

Review today's devotion. What is the Lord telling you? *(Note: It is one thing to have a passing thought; it's another thing to "**dwell**" there.)*

_____

_____

_____

_____

_____

_____

_____

MEMORIZE

Memorize the personalized versions of Philippians 1:2, 6, 9, 18, 21, 27, 2:4-5, 11, 14, 16, 3:8, 14 and 4:6 below, and repeat them every day.

Grace and peace are mine from God my Father and the Lord Jesus Christ.

He who began a good work in me will perfect it until th e day of Christ Jesus.

I will walk in love and righteousness based on real knowledge and discernment of His glory.

As Christ is proclaimed, I will rejoice. For me, to live is Christ, to die is gain!

I will stand firm in one spirit, with one mind, working to further the gospel, thinking of others as more important than myself, having Christ's servant attitude.

That every tongue should confess that Jesus Christ is Lord, to the glory of God the Father.

I will do all without grumbling or disputing, holding fast and holding forth the Word of life.

I will rejoice in the surpassing value of knowing Christ Jesus our Lord.

I will press on toward the goal for the prize of the upward call of God in Christ Jesus.

I will be anxious for nothing, but in everything by prayer and supplication with thanksgiving let my requests be made known to God.

DAY 4
PEACE PRINCIPLES
(continued)

Philippians 4:4-9

4 Rejoice in the Lord always; *again I will say, rejoice!*

    5 Let your forbearing spirit be known to all men. *The Lord is near.*

        6 Be anxious for nothing,

            but **in everything by prayer and supplication with thanksgiving**

                let your requests be made known to God.

            7 *And the* **peace of God,** *(which* **surpasses all comprehension,)**

shall **guard** *your hearts and your minds in Christ Jesus.*

8 *Finally, brethren,*

    whatever is **true,**

        whatever is **honorable,**

            whatever is **right,**

                whatever is **pure,**

                    whatever is **lovely,**

                        whatever is of **good repute,**

                    if there is any **excellence**

                and if anything **worthy of praise,**

        let your mind **dwell** *on these things.*

9 *The things you have* **learned** *and* **received** *and* **heard** *and* **seen** *in me,*

    practice these things; *and the God of peace shall be with you.*

Paul emphasizes, in verse seven, that the peace of God will guard the hearts and minds of Christians, in Jesus. He can only guard, though, that which has been surrendered to Him! Let's take a look at why our hearts and minds need to be protected.

REJOICING AND OUR HEART

The *"heart" (kardia)* refers to the "source and the issues of thought and will,"[110] or the vitality of our life. The heart is the inner system. Following are some verses that speak of the attitude of man's heart.

ACTS 2:46-47
And day by day continuing with one mind in the temple, and breaking bread from house to house, they were taking their meals together with gladness and sincerity of heart, praising God, and having favor with all the people.

Acts 8:22-23

Therefore repent of this wickedness of yours, and pray the Lord that if possible, the intention of your heart may be forgiven you.

Acts 11:23

Then when he had come and witnessed the grace of God, he rejoiced and began to encourage them all with resolute heart to remain true to the Lord;

Acts 13:22

And after He had removed him, He raised up David to be their king, concerning whom He also testified and said, "I have found David the son of Jesse, a man after My heart, who will do all My will."

Acts 15:8-9

And God, who knows the heart, bore witness to them, giving them the Holy Spirit, just as He also did to us; and He made no distinction between us and them, cleansing their hearts by faith.

Acts 28:27

"For the heart of this people has become dull, and with their ears they scarcely hear, and they have closed their eyes; lest they should see with their eyes, and hear with their ears, and understand with their heart and return, and I should heal them."

"Heart" has to do with more than feelings, but is the real inner you. Often the real inner you is veiled, although it is sometimes revealed through your words or actions. What's the condition of YOUR heart?

REJOICING AND OUR MIND

The *"mind" (noêma)* is the source of thought and ideas. The mind has the ability to make decisions. It is the center of human reason and volition in 2 Corinthians 3:14; 4:4.[111]

2 Corinthians 4:4-6

And even if our gospel is veiled, it is veiled to those who are perishing, in whose case the god of this world has blinded the minds of the unbelieving, that they might not see the light of the gospel of the glory of Christ, who is the image of God. For we do not preach ourselves but Christ Jesus as Lord, and ourselves as your bond-servants for Jesus' sake. For God, who said, "Light shall shine out of darkness," is the One who has shone in our hearts to give the light of the knowledge of the glory of God in the face of Christ.

Why does the mind and heart need to be guarded or protected? Essentially, it's this: "an unprotected heart and mind can go off course." Christ has more for us than what we used to be. Essentially then, it's about continuously maintaining our focus, so He can guard our hearts and minds. Maintaining our focus also involves guarding our own minds.

JUDE 20-21
But you, beloved, building yourselves up on your most holy faith; praying in the Holy Spirit; keep yourselves in the love of God, waiting anxiously for the mercy of our Lord Jesus Christ to eternal life.

We choose to "abide" in Him. Unless we guard and allow ourselves to be guarded, we may choose a path that ends up being terribly wrong, or we avoid a good path because it looks hard. We need to guard and be guarded or else the beautiful garden of our life can become nothing more than a bed of weeds or a beaten-down path. Our garden can only be maintained by abiding in Him. Outside of Him, there is no real peace or hope.

REJOICING'S PEACE THOUGHTS: THE POSITIVE THINGS OF THE LORD

The word *finally*, seems to be used by Paul in the sense of "it follows then." Certain "thought life" principles must be followed if we are to have this inner peace from God and maintain a life free of worry (*"Think about such things"*). A person's thoughts determine who he or she is, his or her attitudes and how they act toward others.

What do your thoughts reveal about you? What needs to be changed?

_____

_____

_____

God's Word tells us that our lives are a product of what we think. We are to be careful about what we allow our minds to meditate on. Look up the following verses and summarize them in your own words:

2 Corinthians 10:5 –

Proverbs 23:7 –

Mark 7:20-23 –

**"Sow a thought, reap an action. Sow an action, reap a habit.
Sow a habit, reap a character. Sow a character, reap a destiny!"**

~ Anonymous author

Based on your thought life, what is your destiny?

_____

_____

_____

In Philippians 4:8, the word *"think" (logizomi)* is more than just entertaining thoughts. "This word means *'to evaluate, to calculate, to consider, to weigh or meditate upon.'* The verb form calls for habitual discipline of the mind to set all thoughts on these spiritual virtues. It is a command to obey, not a request to consider."[112]

Define the following terms in your own words. Also, write out an antonym (opposite word) for each.

True –

Honorable –

Right –

Pure –

Lovely –

Good repute –

Worthy of praise –

The charge is to think and practice positive Christ-controlled thinking.

"Whatever is true." True *(alethe)* includes facts and statements that are (1) real (not lies, rumors or embellishments); (2) sincere and genuine (not deceitful or with evil motives); and (3) proper and reliable. God is truth. He speaks only truth.

"Many things in the world seem to be true, but they are not; they are false and deceptive, an illusion and a counterfeit. They seem to offer peace, but what they offer is a deceptive, counterfeit peace—only escapism."[113]

Write some examples.

_____

_____

_____

_____

We are to meditate on things that are true. True relates to the truth of God's Word and the true facts and understandings of daily circumstances, information and feelings. When our thoughts and lives are centered upon true things, we have peace.

Do you need to see truth in a situation you are dealing with right now? What is the truth of that situation?

_____

_____

_____

"Whatever is honorable." Honorable *(semna)* can also be translated as noble, dignified or exalted in character or excellence. Think of someone you could describe as "dignified" or "honorable." What are that person's characteristics?

"Whatever is right." Thoughts and plans that are *right* or *just (dikaios)* meet God's standards of rightness and righteousness. In other words, they are in keeping with the truth. *Right* has to do with right behavior toward man and God.

We are to focus our thoughts upon the things that are *just and righteous.* A mind filled with *just and righteous thoughts* will be a mind that knows peace. Are your current plans *right* or *just?* Is there anything that needs to change in this regard?

"Whatsoever things are pure." Pure *(hagna)* can also be translated as morally clean, spotless, stainless, chaste, undefiled, free from moral pollution, filth, dirt and impurities. As a believer, our mind and thoughts are to be pure. What is God saying to you, right now?

_____

_____

_____

_____

_____

"Whatever is lovely." This is the only place the Greek word for lovely *(prosphiles)* is used in the New Testament. Here, Paul was speaking of thoughts of great moral and spiritual beauty, not of evil. Lovely can also be translated as being pleasing, winsome, kind, gracious; things that excite love and kindness. It's inconsistent with God's principles for the believer to meditate on thoughts of unkindness, meanness, grumbling, murmuring or criticism. "The believer's thoughts are to be focused upon things that are lovely—that build people up, not tear them down."[114]

Is the Lord speaking to you about anything in regard to your thoughts? What is He saying?

_____

_____

_____

_____

_____

"Whatever is commendable." *"Good report (euphemos)* is also translated commendable or admirable. It has to do with things that speak well of the thinker. For example, thoughts that recommend, give confidence in, afford approval or praise, reveal positive and constructive thinking. A believer's thoughts, if heard by others, should be commendable, not condemnatory."[115] In general, we are not to fill our minds with junk!

"If there is any excellence." *Excellence* or *virtue* was commonplace in Greek rhetoric and Roman philosophy, but is used only once in Paul's letters and three times in Peter's (1 Peter 2:9; 2 Peter 1:3, 5). Evidently, Paul brought "virtue" up here to counter the false. This small word incorporates all moral excellence. Paul used this word to sum up all the qualities that could be used to describe a believer's thought life.[116]

"And if there is anything worthy of praise." This phrase may be restated as "anything that deserves the thinker's praise" or "anything that God deems praiseworthy." For believers, who are developing a mind like Christ's, these two should be one and the same.[117]

The source or power for thinking that is *worthy of praise* is two-fold. First, it is the Presence of God. Secondly, it is the Word of God. As we walk in His Spirit, we are convicted of things that are not *of* Him and urged to do things that are pleasing *to* Him. From His Word we are taught about His principles related to thinking, living and acting.

"The things you have learned and received and heard and seen in me; practice these things; and the God of peace shall be with you." The Philippians just had to remember the teachings Paul had given them, what they knew to be true of his life, as well as what they had seen with their own eyes of Paul's conduct. Paul could speak with confidence. People could follow his example because he was following Christ (1 Corinthians 11:1).

Rejoicing and Right Behavior's Result: The Peace of God

When we practice the virtues we just read about, we will experience *the God of peace*. This passage is connected closely to 4:7, *"the peace of God."* "Many people today seek to *have* the peace of God without having to deal *with* God, who is the author of true peace. But that can't be done. To know peace, we must know God."[118]

MEDITATE

Review today's devotion. What is the Lord telling you?

_____

_____

_____

_____

_____

MEMORIZE

Memorize the personalized versions of Philippians 1:2, 6, 9, 18, 21, 27, 2:4-5, 11, 14, 16, 3:8, 14, 4:6 and 8 below, and repeat them every day.

Grace and peace are mine from God my Father and the Lord Jesus Christ.

He who began a good work in me will perfect it until th e day of Christ Jesus.

I will walk in love and righteousness based on real knowledge and discernment of His glory.

As Christ is proclaimed, I will rejoice. For me, to live is Christ, to die is gain!

I will stand firm in one spirit, with one mind, working to further the gospel, thinking of others as more important than myself, having Christ's servant attitude.

That every tongue should confess that Jesus Christ is Lord, to the glory of God the Father.

I will do all without grumbling or disputing, holding fast and holding forth the Word of life.

I will rejoice in the surpassing value of knowing Christ Jesus our Lord.

I will press on toward the goal for the prize of the upward call of God in Christ Jesus.

I will be anxious for nothing, but in everything by prayer and supplication with thanksgiving let my requests be made known to God.

If anything is worthy of praise, I will let my mind dwell on these things.

DAY 5
PEACE WITH CIRCUMSTANCES
Philippians 4:10-23

10 *But I **rejoiced** in the Lord greatly,*

    that now at last you have revived your concern for me;

        indeed, you were concerned before, but you lacked opportunity.

           11 *Not that I speak from want;*

                *for I have learned to be **content** in whatever **circumstances** I am.*

          12 *I know how to get along with **humble means**,*

    *and I also know how to live in **prosperity**; in any and every circumstance*

    *I have learned the **secret of being filled** and **going hungry**,*

        *both of having **abundance** and **suffering need**.*

             13 ***I can do all things through Him who strengthens me**.*

          14 *Nevertheless, you have done well to share with me in my affliction.*

15 *And you yourselves also know, Philippians, that at the first preaching of the gospel,*

        after I departed from Macedonia,

            *no church shared with me in the matter of **giving** and **receiving** but you alone;*

      16 *for even in Thessalonica you sent a gift more than once for my needs.*

            17 *Not that I seek the gift itself, but I seek for the profit which increases to your account.*

              18 *But I have received everything in full, and have an **abundance**;*

    *I am **amply supplied**, having received from Epaphroditus **what you have sent**,*

  *a **fragrant aroma, an acceptable sacrifice, well-pleasing to God**.*

19 *And my God shall supply all your needs according to His riches in glory in Christ Jesus.*

    20 *Now to our God and Father be the glory forever and ever. Amen.*

        21 *Greet every saint in Christ Jesus. The brethren who are with me greet you.*

    22 *All the saints greet you, especially those of Caesar's household.*

23 *The **grace** of the Lord Jesus Christ be with your spirit.*

How can Paul, a man who has been through so much, have peace and contentment? It defies the realm of reason! After all, one must have peaceful circumstances to have peace. If we just had more money or a better spouse, child or parent, then we would be content! Well, maybe not.

In this chapter, Paul describes wonderful spiritual resources that make us adequate in any circumstance and give us peace and contentment.

PAUL'S CONFIDENCE IN GOD'S PROVIDENCE (4:10)

Though twelve years had passed, the Philippians had not forgotten Paul's service among them. They were concerned when they received word that he was now imprisoned in Rome and lacked everything. Friends had left him. He could not work to support himself. Very likely he was cold during the long months of the damp Roman winter. Immediately, the Philippians began to collect funds. For a while, opportunity to send the gift had been lacking. As soon as this situation changed, the Philippians had sent the gift to Rome in the care of Epaphroditus. Paul was overjoyed. In the closing words of this letter he wrote, *"I rejoice greatly in the Lord that at last you have renewed your concern for me. Indeed, you have been concerned, but you had no opportunity to show it."*

Paul was pleased about the gift that the Philippians had sent not only for his own sake, but for their sake. For he knew that a gift actually benefits the giver more than it benefits the one who receives it. Their gift was a *"fragrant offering, an acceptable sacrifice, pleasing to God"* (Philippians 4:10–14, 17-18).

With these words, Paul assured the saints that he knew how to live on a very small income. In his rejoicing, Paul wanted to make clear that he was not asking for more gifts and acknowledged God's care in the midst of all his circumstances, both good and bad. He had learned to be content.

"Life is not a series of accidents; it is a series of appointments."[119] *"I will guide thee with Mine eye"* (Psalm 32:8 KJV). Abraham called God "Jehovah-Jireh," meaning "the Lord will see to it" (Genesis 22:14). *"And when He putteth forth His own sheep, He goeth before them"* (John 10:4 KJV).

Though we can see the result of God's providence, we do not know how He causes it to occur. For this reason God's providence appears mysterious to us. God simply does not tell us some things about His providence (and other matters, Deuteronomy 29:29). *"O the depth of the riches both of the wisdom and knowledge of God! How unsearchable are His judgments, and His ways past finding out!"* (Romans 11:33). In spite of the mysterious aspect of His providence, it is a wonderful source of confident contentment.

Look up the following passages and summarize what each had to do with God's providence:

Psalm 121:3 –

Genesis 45:4-8 –

Matthew 10:28-31 –

Romans 8:28 –

Reflect on some past situations where you have seen God's providence in your life. List them below.

_____

_____

_____

_____

It would be good to talk about God's wonderful providence in your life with significant people. Give praise to God for the wondrous things He has done. Giving testimony is a wonderful way to share your faith with others, both Christians and non-Christians. Next time you are tempted to dwell on the negative aspects of a circumstance, think on God's providence and faithfulness in the past.

PAUL'S RELIANCE ON GOD'S PREVAILING POWER (4:11–13)

Jesus teaches this same lesson in the sermon on the vine and branches in John 15. There He tells us, *"I am the Vine and you are the branches."* A branch has one purpose: to bear fruit. Otherwise, it might as well be burned. "The branch does not bear fruit through its own self-effort, but by drawing on the life of the Vine."[120] *"Without Me, you can do nothing"* (John 15:5). As the believer maintains his communion with Christ, the power of God is there to see him through. *"I am self-sufficient in Christ's sufficiency"* (Philippians 4:13).[121]

"The words *'have learned'* speak of entrance into a new condition."[122] Paul had grown up in luxury, and had never gone without as a young man. It was only after his conversion that he had learned to be content in the midst of whatever life threw at him. His joy came from something deep within and had nothing to do with his condition, whether it be one of poverty or prosperity. He had been meticulously established in the mystery of contentment by a work of the Holy Spirit as he experienced life. This mystery is only revealed to those who fear God (Psalm 25:14). Those who reject Christ are mystified by the ability of Christ-surrendered Christians to remain calm in trouble and humble in prosperity.

"Content" (*autarkēs*, sufficient) means "to be independent of external circumstances."[123] In the NT the word is represented as part of godliness (1 Timothy 6:6). Paul's contentment in Philippians 4:11 is centered in *"Christ who strengthens me"* (v. 13). *" 'Enough'* also means having something to give to others too (2 Corinthians 9:8).[124] Paul's conversion experience and trials for Christ had taught him to say, "The path which I traveled led me ever closer to Christ, to His love, and to His power, yes to Christ and *contentment* in Him. That very contentment is riches to me."[125]

Compare the difficulty of your situation with Paul's. What is difficult? What do you have to be thankful for?

_____

_____

_____

Paul is no emotionless stone statue. He is a real man, who knows both happy and sad situations, yet is content. This *contentment* or soul-sufficiency (see also 1 Timothy 6:6) is not self-manufactured. Christ is his Source of strength and sufficiency. He is able to be independent of circumstances because he is dependent upon Christ.

Again and again Paul had been humbled (brought low) by crises circumstances. He personally had experienced hunger, thirst, fasting, cold, nakedness, physical suffering, mental torture, persecution, beatings, etc. (see Acts 14:19; Acts 16:22-25; Acts 17:13; Acts 18:12; Acts 20:3). He had peace because his contentment did not come from circumstances or things. It came from Christ alone!

It's natural to fall to our knees in prayer when circumstances have brought us low. In difficulty and trouble we immediately recognize our own inadequacy. It's less natural to humbly rely on the Lord in times of prosperity. Prosperity can soften spiritual passion and defuse Christ-focused living. *"I am rich, and increased with goods, and have need of nothing"* (Revelation 3:17). The person whose focus is turned to "things" will be a discontented person, because the "things" of this world cannot satisfy. Yet Paul was able to say, *"I have learned the secret of being filled and going hungry, both of having abundance and suffering need"* (v. 12).

The words *"to abound"* are from a Greek word which means "to overflow;" "over and above;" "more than enough."[126] The words *"to be full"* are from a very strong Greek word. It was used of the feeding of animals. In this passage, it means, "to be filled" and so "to fatten like an animal;" "to be satiated.[127] A *"satiated"* person is often a discontented person. In comparison, Paul knew what it was to live on a little, and he knew how to have more than he could use. He knew how to be satiated, yet content.

Contentment was something that was obscure (*a secret*) to Paul, as a Pharisee, living a constant life of plenty. Before his conversion, Paul had been a person of prestige. His future looked bright and he lived a life of plenty. Yet, he had lacked the "pearl of great price" (salvation) and a Christ-centered peace of soul. His zealous works of the flesh had left him empty. After his conversion, there had also been periods of time when he had experienced what it meant to have plenty (Acts 16:15, 40; Acts 16:33-34; Acts 20:11; Acts 28:2; Philippians 4:15-16, 18), yet it was combined with peace and contentment. Now, it is not always easy to carry oneself well in the midst of plenty (Proverbs 30:8; Mark 10:23-25). As someone once said, "In order to carry a full cup, one must have a steady hand." It is Christ who steadies the hand.

In your times of plenty, have you kept your focus on Christ? What is Christ saying to you now?

_____

_____

_____

In every circumstance, Paul is able to enthusiastically proclaim, *"I can do all things in Him who infuses strength into me."*[128] Paul can do whatever he needs to do, for he is *in Christ* (Philippians 3:9), in vital union and intimate fellowship with his Lord and Savior. "The cross was more than a chain worn around his neck. It was burned into his life!"[129] Christ was in him and he lived and walked in Christ. Read some of Paul's writings below:

2 Corinthians 12:9-10

And He has said to me, "My grace is sufficient for you, for power is perfected in weakness." Most gladly, therefore, I will rather boast about my weaknesses, so that the power of Christ may dwell in me. Therefore I am well content with weaknesses, with insults, with distresses, with persecutions, with difficulties, for Christ's sake; for when I am weak, then I am strong.

2 Timothy 4:16-18

At my first defense no one supported me, but all deserted me; may it not be counted against them. But the Lord stood with me and strengthened me, so that through me the proclamation might be fully accomplished, and that all the Gentiles might hear; and I was rescued out of the lion's mouth. The Lord will rescue me from every evil deed, and will bring me safely to His heavenly kingdom; to Him be the glory forever and ever. Amen.

Philippians 4:13

"I can do all things in Him who strengthens me."

"I can" (ischuô)

> To be: capable of ... strong ... healthy ... have power.[130]

"Strengtheneth" (endunamoô)

> More literally, infuses strength into me, as the old verb inforce.[131]

An Amplified translation of 4:12-13: *"I know in fact how to keep myself low; I know in fact how to have more than enough. In everything and in all things I have learned the secret, both to be satiated and to be hungry, and to have more than enough and to lack. I am strong for all things in the One who constantly infuses strength in me."*[132]

Paul was able to walk in peace and contentment because he had confidence in God's providence and relied on God's power. Christ was in him and he lived and walked *in Christ*. God knows what is and what is to come. Worrying changes nothing. Prayer releases a power that can change even the most difficult situation.

Contentment is not escape from the battle, but peace in the midst of the battle. In closing, Paul said of his beloved friends:

Philippians 4:18-20

But I have received everything in full, and have an abundance; I am amply supplied, having received from Epaphroditus what you have sent, a fragrant aroma, an acceptable sacrifice, well-pleasing to God. And my God shall supply all your needs according to His riches in glory in Christ Jesus. Now to our God and Father be the glory forever and ever. Amen.

MEDITATE

Re-read the above devotion. Meditate on its meaning for your life. Write your thoughts below.

_____

_____

_____

_____

_____

_____

MEMORIZE

Memorize the personalized versions of Philippians 1:2, 6, 9, 18, 21, 27, 2:4-5, 11, 14, 16, 3:8, 14, 4:6, 8 and 13 below, and repeat them every day.

Grace and peace are mine from God my Father and the Lord Jesus Christ.

He who began a good work in me will perfect it until th e day of Christ Jesus.

I will walk in love and righteousness based on real knowledge and discernment of His glory.

As Christ is proclaimed, I will rejoice. For me, to live is Christ, to die is gain!

I will stand firm in one spirit, with one mind, working to further the gospel, thinking of others as more important than myself, having Christ's servant attitude.

That every tongue should confess that Jesus Christ is Lord, to the glory of God the Father.

I will do all without grumbling or disputing, holding fast and holding forth the Word of life.

I will rejoice in the surpassing value of knowing Christ Jesus our Lord.

I will press on toward the goal for the prize of the upward call of God in Christ Jesus.

I will be anxious for nothing, but in everything by prayer and supplication with thanksgiving let my requests be made known to God.

If anything is worthy of praise, I will let my mind dwell on these things.

I can do all things in Him who strengthens me.

And my God shall supply all my needs according to His riches in Glory in Christ Jesus.

SUMMARY

Paul's mad world bares some striking resemblance to our own. The Apostles mad world was made up of people—sinful and lost. Likewise, our communities, cities, states and nations are made up of people. The best way to change nations is to change people … one by one.

God has left the Church in the world to serve as an agent of change by lighting the darkness with His truth … by lifting Him up so that nations can be impacted in a positive way.

The problem is that the Church has often allowed itself to be darkened by falsehood as it has allowed the world's philosophies to overshadow God's truth.

Not only nations, but the Church is made up of people, like you and I. The Church is not a building, but a community of believers. The only way for you and I as Christians to shine as lights in the darkness, is to live and walk the life of surrender. In Paul's life we see an example of what this looks like and how it can be done.

So, friend, allow the revolution to continue in your life. Walk in **Surrender's Transformation, Joy and Destiny**. Allow Him to make you a light in the darkness, a reflection of His glory, so that men will be drawn to Him. Daily continue to speak forth the personalized scripture proclamation you have been repeating until those words drive your thoughts and actions. Change in the Church and in this world starts and continues with people. Let it start and continue with you. *Shine … shine … shine!*

Watch for more **Upward Living** resources to help you grow in your Christian walk and impact. All resources are designed to be used individually and in groups, by men, women and youth. They are great resources to be used for all church studies.

Be sure to review *Upward Living: Surrender's Walk*, which may be used by itself or as a companion to *Upward Living in a World Gone Mad*.

God bless you and keep you as you shine for Him!

Footnotes
(Endnotes)

[1] Tacitus 14.1-11; Dio 62.11-14. *An Online Encyclopedia of Roman Rulers.* (cited 2 February 2009). Available on the internet: http://roman-emperors.org/nero.htm#N_2_. Used by permission.

[2] Ibid.

[3] Ibid.

[4] Galba criticized Nero's *luxuria,* both his public and private excessive spending, during rebellion, Tacitus, *Annals* I.16; Kragelund, Patrick, "Nero's Luxuria, in Tacitus and in the Octavia," *The Classical Quarterly,* 2000, p. 494-515. Used by permission.

[5] Nero did not play a fiddle, but a lyre. Suetonius claimed that Nero played the lyre while Rome burned. See Suetonius, *The Lives of Twelve Caesars,* Life of Nero. A detailed explanation of this transition is given in M.F. Gyles "Nero Fiddled while Rome Burned." *The Classical Journal* (1948), p. 211-217. Used by permission.

[6] Tacitus 15.38-44, Suetonius 38. See "Beaujeu, Freudenberger, Wlosok." *An Online Encyclopedia of Roman Rulers.* (cited 2 February 2009). Available on the Internet: http://roman-emperors.org/nero.htm#N_2_. Used by permission.

[7] Viscount, James Bryce. *Studies in History and Jurisprudence* (New York: Oxford University Press, 1901). 2 vols. The Online Library of Liberty. (cited 1 January 2009). Available on the Internet: http://oll.libertyfund.org/?option=com_staticxt&staticfile=show.php%3Ftitle=2004&chapter=138477&layout=html&Itemid=27. Used by permission.

[8] John T. Bristow, *What Paul Really Said About Women,* (HarperOne, 1991) p. 98-99. Used by permission.

[9] Ibid.

[10] Tertullian *Nat.* 11; *De An.* 37-39; Augustine *Civ.* D. 4.11.

[11] Gerald F. Hawthorne, Ralph P. Martin, Daniel G. Reid, ed., *Dictionary of Paul and His Letters,* (Downers Grove, IL: InterVarsity Press, 1993.) Used by permission.

[12] Josephus J.W. 2.16.4 §§345–401.

[13] *Mart. Pol.* 3.2; Justin Martyr, *Apol. I* 6; *Apol. II* 3.

[14] Craig A. Evans and Stanley E. Porter, "Persecution," in *Dictionary of New Testament Background,* (Downers Grove, IL: InterVarsity Press, 2000). Used by permission.

[15] Hawthorne, op. cit.

[16] *Thayer's Greek Lexicon,* Electronic Database. (San Jose: Biblesoft, Inc., 2000, 2003). Used by permission.

[17] Ibid.

[18] *Greek-English Lexicon Based on Semantic Domain.* (New York: United Bible Societies, 1988). Used by permission.

[19] Billy Graham, *Peace With God.* (Nashville: Word Publishing, 1984) p. 215. Used by permission.

[20] Evans, Des. Teaching Series on the Book of Philippians (taped), 1985. Used by permission.

[21] *Greek-English Lexicon Based on Semantic Domain,* op. cit.

[22] *UBS Handbook Series* (United Bible Societies, 1961-1997). Used by permission.

[23] From *Greek-English Lexicon Based on Semantic Domain,* op. cit.

[24] *Vine's Expository Dictionary of Biblical Words,* Copyright © 1985, Thomas Nelson Publishers. Used by permission.

[25] *Thayer's Greek Lexicon,* Electronic Database. Copyright © 2000, 2003 by Biblesoft, Inc. All rights reserved. Used by permission.

[26] *Greek-English Lexicon Based on Semantic Domain,* op. cit.

[27] *Thayers,* op. cit.

[28] *Greek-English Lexicon Based on Semantic Domain,* op. cit.

[29] *Vine's Expository Dictionary of Biblical Words,* op. cit.

[30] *Greek-English Lexicon Based on Semantic Domain,* op. cit.

[31] *Thayer's Greek Lexicon,* op. cit.

[32] *Vine's Expository Dictionary of Biblical Words,* op. cit.

[33] Evans, Des, Teaching Series on the Book of Philippians (taped), 1985. Used by permission.

[34] Ibid.

[35] Ibid.

[36] Ibid.

[37] Ibid.

38 *Vine's Expository Dictionary of Biblical Words*, op. cit.

39 *The American Heritage® Dictionary of the English Language,* Fourth Edition. (Houghton Mifflin Company, 2007). All rights reserved. Used by permission.

40 *Wikipedia.* This article is licensed under the GNU Free Documentation License. It uses material from the Wikipedia article "Opinion." Available on the internet: wikipedia.org. Used by permission.

41 *Thayer's,* Ibid.

42 Definition of "Discernment," (cited 15 December 2008). Available on the internet: wordnet.princeton.edu/perl/webwn, Used by permission.

43 *Webster's Dictionary.* Definition of "Discernment," (cited 15 December 2008). Available on the internet: http://merriam-webster.com/dictionary/discernment. Used by permission.

44 *Greek-English Lexicon Based on Semantic Domain*, op. cit.

45 Wuest, Kenneth S. Wuest's *Word Studies – Volume 2: Word Studies in the Greek New Testament,* (Grand Rapids, MI: Wm. B. Eerdmans, 1973). Used by permission.

46 *Thayer's,* Ibid.

47 Des Evans, op. cit.

48 Des Evans, op. cit.

49 Des Evans, op. cit.

50 A 2005 study of faith and spirituality in America, (Accessed in 3 June 2007). Was available on the internet: http://barna.org, Used by permission.

51 *UBS Handbook Series,* (United Bible Societies, 1961-1997). Used by permission.

52 Evans, Des, op. cit.

53 Evans, Des, op. cit.

54 Kenneth S. Wuest, *Wuest's Word Studies – Volume 2: Word Studies in the Greek New Testament,* (Grand Rapids, MI: Wm. B. Eerdmans, 1973), WORD*search* CROSS e-book, 51. Used by permission.

55 Evans, Des, op. cit.

56 Wuest, Ibid.

57 Evans, Des, op. cit.

58 Evans, Des, op. cit.

59 *UBS Handbook Series*, op. cit.

60 *Greek-English Lexicon based on Semantic Domain*, op. cit.

61 Ibid.

62 *Persecution of Christians On the Rise Worldwide*, ACN Report Reveals, 11/10/2008 - 10:11 AM PST. Available on the internet: http://catholic.org/prwire/headline.php?ID=5331. Used by permission.

63 *Thayer's Greek Lexicon*, Electronic Database. Copyright © 2000, 2003 by Biblesoft, Inc. All rights reserved. Used by permission.

64 *Vine's Expository Dictionary of Biblical Words*, op. cit.

65 *USB Handbook Series*, op. cit.

66 Ibid.

67 Ibid.

68 *Thayer's*, op. cit.

69 Evans, Des, op. cit.

70 Rod Mattoon, *Mattoon's Treasures – Treasures from Philippians*, (Springfield, IL: Lincoln Land Baptist Church, n.d.), WORD search CROSS e-book, 51. Used by permission.

71 Wuest, op. cit, p. 51.

72 Ibid, p. 71-70.

73 *Robertson's Word Pictures in the New Testament*, Electronic Database. Copyright © 1997, 2003 by Biblesoft, Inc. Robertson's Word Pictures in the New Testament. Copyright © 1985 by Broadman Press. Used by permission.

74 *Adam Clarke's Commentary*, Electronic Database (San Jose: Biblesoft, Inc., 1996, 2003). All rights reserved. Used by permission.

75 Wuest, op. cit.

76 Geoffrey W. Bromiley, trans., Gerhard Kittel, Gerhard Friedrich, ed., *Theological Dictionary of the New Testament: Abridged in One Volume,* (Grand Rapids, MI: William B. Eerdmans, 2003), s.v., WORD*search* CROSS e-book. Used by permission.

77 Evans, Des, op. cit.

78   "Timothy" research (6 February 2009). Available on the internet: http://en.wikipedia.org/wiki/Timothy. Used by permission.

79   "Timothy" research (6 February 2009). Available on the internet: http://bible.org/page.php?page_id=1441. Used by permission.

80   Evans, Des, op. cit.

81   *Greek-English Lexicon Based on Semantic Domain*, op. cit.

82   Evans, Des, op. cit.

83   Ibid.

84   Ibid.

85   "Ancient Olympic Games" *(Microsoft Encarta Online Encyclopedia, 2006)*. Microsoft Corporation (1997-20-06). Retrieved on 2006-12-27. Used by permission.

86   "Olympics." Available on the internet: http://museum.upenn.edu/new/olympics/olympicfaqs.shtml. Retrieved on 2008-12-27. Retrieved on 2008-1-09. Used by permission.

87   "Olympics." Available on the internet: http://ancienthistory.about.com/b/2008/08/11/what-was-the-training-like-for-the-ancient-olympics.htm. Public domain translation. Retrieved on 2008-1-09. Used by permission.

88   "Olympics." (Retrieved on 2009-1-09) Available on the internet: http://ancienthistory.about.com/od/olympics/tp/073008OlympicCheats.htm. Used by permission.

89   http://copacabanarunners.net/ihistolimpia.html. Retrieved 2008-12-27. Used by permission.

90   *Adam Clarke's Commentary*, op. cit.

91   *Strong's Talking Greek & Hebrew Dictionary*. Used by permission.

92   *Adam Clarke's Commentary*, op. cit.

93   Evans, Des, op. cit.

94   Wuest, op. cit.

95   Ibid.

96   Ibid.

97   "Firm," (Retrieved 15 January 2009). Available on the internet: http://thefreedictionary.com/stand. Used by permission.

98   "Firm," (Retrieved 15 January 2009). Available on the internet: Wordnet.princeton.edu/perl/webwn. Used by permission.

99   "Firm," (Retrieved 15 January 2009). Available on the internet: http://thefreedictionary.com/firm. Used by permission.

100 Gordon D. Fee, *The IVP New Testament Commentary Series – Philippians*, ed. Grant R. Osborne (Downers Grove, IL: InterVarsity Press, 1999), WORD*search* CROSS e-book, 167-169. Used by permission.

101 Ibid.

102 *The American Heritage® Dictionary of the English Language*, (Houghton Mifflin Company, 2000, 2003). All rights reserved. Available on the internet: http://thefreedictionary.com/HARMONY. Used by permission.

103 Barclay, William. *Barclay's Daily Study Bible (NT)*, WORD*search* CROSS e-book, Under: "Chapter 4". Used by permission.

104 Bruce B. Barton et al., *Life Application Bible Commentary – Philippians, Colossians, & Philemon*, (Wheaton, IL: Tyndale, 1995), WORD*search* CROSS e-book, 113. Used by permission.

105 Wuest, op. cit, under: "Verse 5."

106 Bruce B. Barton et al., *Life Application Bible Commentary – Philippians, Colossians, & Philemon*, (Wheaton, IL: Tyndale, 1995), WORD*search* CROSS e-book, 116-117. Used by permission.

107 Ibid.

108 Ibid, p.115.

109 Ibid, p. 116-117.

110 Marvin R. Vincent, *Word Studies in the New Testament*, (New York: Scribners, 1887), WORD*search* CROSS e-book, Under: "Philippians 4:7." Used by permission.

111 Stephen D. Renn, *Expository Dictionary of Bible Words: Word Studies for Key English Bible Words Based on the Hebrew and Greek Texts*, (Peabody, MA: Hendrickson Pub., 2005), s.v. "MIND," WORD*search* CROSS e-book. Used by permission.

112 Mattoon, Ron. *Mattoon's Treasures – Treasures from Philippians*, (Springfield, IL: Lincoln Land Baptist Church, n.d.), WORD*search* CROSS e-book, 219. Used by permission.

113 *The Preacher's Outline & Sermon Bible – Galatians, Ephesians, Philippians, Colossians*, (Chattanooga: Leadership Ministries Worldwide, 1991), WORD*search* CROSS e-book, Under: "B. The Steps to Peace (Part II): Prayer and Positive Thinking, 4:6-9." Used by permission.

114 Ibid.

115 Bruce B. Barton et al., *Life Application Bible Commentary – Philippians, Colossians, & Philemon*, (Wheaton, IL: Tyndale, 1995), WORD*search* CROSS e-book, 117-119. Used by permission.

116 Ibid.

117 Ibid.

118 Ibid, p. 119.

119 Warren W. Wiersbe, *The Bible Exposition Commentary – New Testament, Volume 2,* (Colorado Springs, CO: Victor, 2001), WORD*search* CROSS e-book, p. 97. Used by permission.

120 Ibid, p. 98.

121 Ibid.

122 Kenneth S. Wuest, *Wuest's Word Studies – Volume 2: Word Studies in the Greek New Testament,* (Grand Rapids, MI: Wm. B. Eerdmans, 1973), WORD*search* CROSS e-book, 112-113. Used by permission.

123 Ibid.

124 Geoffrey W. Bromiley, trans., Gerhard Kittel, Gerhard Friedrich, ed., *Theological Dictionary of the New Testament: Abridged in One Volume,* (Grand Rapids, MI: William B. Eerdmans, 2003), s.v., WORD*search* CROSS e-book. Used by permission.

125 Hendriksen, William. *Baker New Testament Commentary – Exposition of Galatians, Ephesians, Philippians, Colossians, and Philemon,* (Grand Rapids, MI: Baker Academic, 2007), WORD*search* CROSS e-book, p. 203-206. Used by permission.

126 Zodhiates, Spiros. *The Complete Word Study Dictionary – New Testament,* (Chattanooga, TN: AMG Publishers, 1993), WORDsearch CROSS e-book, Under: "pe??ss??". Used by permission.

127 Ibid.

128 *Vincent's New Testament Word Studies, 4 Volumes* by Marvin R. Vincent <http://christianbook.com/Christian/Books/search?author=Marvin> /Hendrickson Publishers / 1886 Used by permission.

129 Evans, Des, op. cit.

130 Johannes P. Louw and Eugene A. Nida, *Greek-English Lexicon of the New Testament: Based on Symantic Domain,* (New York: United Bible Societies, 1989), WORD*search* CROSS e-book, Under: Philippians 4:13. Used by permission.

131 Marvin R. Vincent, *Word Studies in the New Testament,* (New York: Scribners, 1887), WORDsearch CROSS e-book, Under: "Philippians 4:13." Used by permission.

132 Wuest, op. cit., p. 113-114.

www.ingramcontent.com/pod-product-compliance
Lightning Source LLC
Chambersburg PA
CBHW081329090426

42737CB00017B/3071